The
Soccer
Encyclopedia

FIFA Official Licenced Publication

This is a Welbeck Children's book
Text, design, and illustration copyright © Welbeck Publishing Limited 2021
Published in 2021 by Welbeck Books Limited an imprint of the
Welbeck Publishing Group, 20 Mortimer Street, London W1T 3JW

A catalogue record is available for this book from the Library of Congress.
10 9 8 7 6 5 4 3 2 1
ISBN 978 1 78312 571 5

Printed and bound in Italy
Author: Emily Stead
Editor: Suhel Ahmed
Designer: RockJaw Creative
Design Manager: Matt Drew
Picture research: Paul Langan
Production: Arlene Alexander

PRIMARY SOURCE REFERENCES:

Federation Internationale de
Football Association (FIFA)
www.fifa.com

Union of European Football Associations (UEFA)
www.uefa.com

Confederation of North, Central American, and Caribbean
Association Football (CONCACAF)
www.concacaf.com

Confederación Sudamericana de Fútbol (CONMEBOL)
www.conmebol.com

Confédération Africaine de Football (CAF)
www.cafonline.com

Asian Football Confederation (AFC)
www.the-afc.com

Oceania Football Confederation
https://www.oceaniafootball.com/

The Football Association (FA)
www.thefa.com

Encyclopaedia Britannica
https://www.britannica.com/sports/football-soccer

BBC Sport Football
www.bbc.co.uk/sport/football
https://www.bbc.co.uk/sport/football/womens

International Federation of Football History and Statistics
https://iffhs.de/

Guinness World Records
https://www.guinnessworldrecords.com/

The Rec.Sport.Soccer Statistics Foundation
www.rsssf.com

The
Soccer
Encyclopedia

FIFA Official Licenced Publication

WELBECK

CONTENTS

THE EVOLUTION OF SOCCER

Simple ball games have existed for thousands of years. But it was not until the middle of the nineteenth century that the rules of soccer were written down, giving rise to the game as we know it today. Currently, more than four billion fans (more than half of the planet's population) regularly cheer on their teams around the world.

Close-up action shot from the FIFA World Cup Russia 2018™ group game between Morocco and Iran.

THE ORIGINS OF SOCCER

Although modern soccer began in Great Britain, many other versions of the game existed thousands of years earlier on different continents. These ancient ball games helped to shape soccer's evolution, playing an important role in its history.

1600 BCE

ANCIENT BALL GAME

The first recorded team sport involving a ball was played by the Maya and Aztecs. Players scored by moving a solid rubber ball to either end of a sloped, stone court. If a player managed to pass the ball through a stone hoop in the middle of the court, they would be hailed the victor.

800 BCE

GREEK GAME

Episkyros was played in Greece as early as 800 BCE. While players (12 on each team) used their hands to move the ball, many rules of the game were similar to those of soccer. The game was played on a field marked with white lines.

200 BCE

CUJU IN CHINA

The first game in which players had to kick a ball was a Chinese invention that was first played more than 2,000 years ago. The game, called *tsu'chu* or *cuju*, used a leather ball tightly stuffed with feathers. Players had to score without using their hands or arms.

The Chinese ancient ball game *cuju* may have been used as a training exercise for soldiers during the Han dynasty (206 BCE–CE 220).

146 BCE

ROMAN HARPASTUM

After conquering Greece, the Romans borrowed the ball games of the ancient Greeks and came up with their own version called *harpastum*. The biggest rule change the Romans introduced was that players were allowed to kick the ball.

Nineteenth century depiction of two teams from an English boarding school playing the "field game"— an early version of soccer.

1863

THE FOOTBALL ASSOCIATION

In October 1863, an important event took place in London that would change the course of soccer history. When the English Football Association (FA) was formed, it wrote down the game's first set of rules. The FA decided that players could no longer carry the ball with their hands, and, among other things, agreed that a standard size and weight of ball should be used.

1800s

SCHOOL SPORTS

Games that combined parts of modern rugby and soccer became popular at British boarding schools in the nineteenth century. The rules were different at each school, so it was impossible for teams to play each other fairly. Attempts to create official guidelines failed, because the schools couldn't agree on a uniform set of rules.

1070–1400

MOB FOOTBALL

"Mob football" was played in England in medieval times. Teams had to kick and punch a ball made from an inflated pig's bladder along the village roads! The "fields" could be miles long and games attracted scrums of players. Games often caused injury and were soon outlawed for being too violent.

GROWING THE GAME

The first major soccer competition in the world, The FA Cup, was played in 1871–72, while the first league championship kicked off soon after. Support for the sport spread and games began to attract huge crowds. Many teams had to build large stadiums to fit in the growing number of fans.

In 1889, Preston North End earned the nickname "The Invincibles" after going through the entire 22–game league competition unbeaten.

FOOTBALL FIRSTS

1872 **INTERNATIONAL MATCH** — Scotland v. England

1872 **FA CUP WINNERS** — Wanderers FC

1889 **FOOTBALL LEAGUE CHAMPIONSHIP WINNERS** — Preston North End

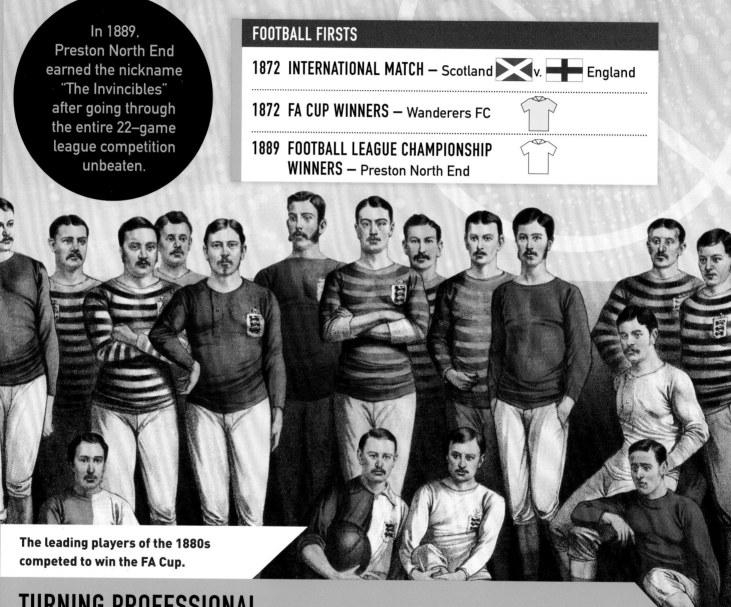

The leading players of the 1880s competed to win the FA Cup.

TURNING PROFESSIONAL

Initially, the FA forbade clubs from paying players. As a result, English teams such as Preston North End used money from ticket sales to cover their players' expenses. Pressure from teams and players then forced the FA to change the rule in 1885 and a maximum wage limit was imposed from 1893 until 1945. The FA finally ended wage restrictions in 1961, when players threatened to strike if they were not paid their "true worth."

TOP TRANSFERS

Aston Villa paid 100 British pounds ($125) in 1893 for the transfer of Willie Groves from West Bromwich Albion. Since then, a lot has changed. In the modern game, players swap teams for eye-watering sums during two transfer windows—in the summer and winter. In 2017, Paris Saint-Germain made history by smashing the record transfer price, paying $250 million for FC Barcelona star Neymar.

Forward Willie Groves (circled), as a West Bromwich Albion player.

Brazilian Neymar is unveiled as Paris Saint-Germain's premier signing in 2017.

RECORD-BREAKING TRANSFERS

ESTIMATED TRANSFER SUM	DATE	PLAYER	FROM	TO
$ 125	1893	WILLIE GROVES	WEST BROMWICH ALBION	ASTON VILLA
$ 1,250	1905	ALF COMMON	SUNDERLAND	MIDDLESBROUGH TOWN
$ 12,500	1928	DAVID JACK	BOLTON WANDERERS	ARSENAL
$ 125,000	1961	LUIS SUÁREZ	FC BARCELONA	FC INTERNAZIONALE
$ 1,250,000	1975	GIUSEPPE SAVOLDI	BOLOGNA FC	SSC NAPOLI
$ 12,250,000	1992	JEAN PIERRE-PAPIN	OLYMPIQUE DE MARSEILLE	AC MILAN
$ 250,000,000	2017	NEYMAR	FC BARCELONA	PARIS SAINT-GERMAIN

GOING GLOBAL

Soccer's popularity took off after the sport became professional. At the turn of the twentieth century, soldiers, sailors, and railroad builders introduced the beautiful game as they traveled to countries across the British Empire. People fell in love with soccer across Europe and elsewhere from Central and South America to Africa, which led countries to form their own soccer associations.

A sketch of a soccer game (the 59th Regiment v. the Garrison), in Candahar (Kandahar), Afghanistan in 1892.

SOCCER AROUND THE WORLD

FIFA is the organization in charge of soccer worldwide. As well as looking after the FIFA World Cup™, the FIFA Women's World Cup™, and other soccer competitions, FIFA's role is to make sure that people everywhere can join in the world's most popular sport. "FIFA" stands for Fédération Internationale de Football Association, and was founded in Paris in 1904. Today, FIFA has 211 national member associations across six continents. Each continent has its own regional confederation.

CONCACAF

Formed in 1961, Concacaf organizes soccer in North America, Central America, and the Caribbean. It has forty-one members from Canada to the Caribbean.

⚽ MAJOR COMPETITIONS

International: Concacaf Gold Cup
Concacaf Nations League
Concacaf Women's Championship

Club: Concacaf Champions League
Concacaf League

CONMEBOL

CONMEBOL is the oldest regional federation, founded in 1916. It governs soccer in South America and consists of ten members.

⚽ MAJOR COMPETITIONS

International: CONMEBOL Copa América
CONMEBOL Copa América Femenina

Club: CONMEBOL Copa Libertadores
CONMEBOL Copa Libertadores Femenina
CONMEBOL Copa Sudamericana

adidas
Tricolore 19
OFFICIAL MATCH BALL

MAJOR COMPETITIONS	FOUNDED	MOST SUCCESSFUL TEAMS	
FIFA WORLD CUP™	1930	BRAZIL (five titles)	★★★★★
FIFA WOMEN'S WORLD CUP™	1991	USA (four titles)	★★★★

UEFA

UEFA is the organization in charge of soccer in Europe. Founded in 1954, it currently has fifty-five members.

⚽ MAJOR COMPETITIONS

International: UEFA European Championship
UEFA Nations League

Club: UEFA Champions League
UEFA Europa League
UEFA Women's Champions League

AFC

The AFC organizes soccer in Asia and Australia. It was formed in 1954 and has forty-seven members.

⚽ MAJOR COMPETITIONS

International: AFC Asian Cup
AFC Women's Asian Cup

Club: AFC Champions League

OFC

The OFC is the governing body for soccer in Oceania. It is the youngest and smallest of all six confederations. Formed in 1966, it has fourteen members.

⚽ MAJOR COMPETITIONS

International: OFC Nations Cup
OFC Women's Nations Cup

Club: OFC Champions League

CAF

Founded in 1957, CAF is Africa's governing body and has fifty-six members—the most of all the confederations.

⚽ MAJOR COMPETITIONS

International: Africa Cup of Nations
Africa Women's Cup of Nations

Club: CAF Champions League
CAF Confederations Cup

WOMEN'S SOCCER

The history of the women's game is full of many highs and lows. Nowadays, more than 30 million women around the world take part in the sport, but they were once banned from playing in numerous countries. Many have had to fight hard over the last century to help women's soccer grow into the exciting game we know today.

THE WORLD AT WAR

Up until World War I broke out across Europe in 1914, both the men's and women's games had been growing in the United Kingdom, attracting large crowds. As men left to fight overseas, women took on their roles in weapons factories, offices, and farming. The British government supported women's teams—both for the health of the women and to keep up morale at home.

Action from the final of the 2019 FIFA Women's World Cup™ between the USA and the Netherlands.

Dick, Kerr Ladies FC lost just 28 of the 833 games they played from 1917 to 1965.

A GOLDEN AGE

Dick, Kerr Ladies FC was formed at a munitions factory in Preston, England. Led by their ferocious forward, Lily Parr, the team's popularity grew thanks to their impressive performances. Even after the war, the team continued to attract record crowds of up to 53,000 supporters. Then, in 1921, The FA prohibited women from playing at their grounds, claiming the sport was "quite unsuitable for females." The resulting ban lasted fifty years, as other countries followed England's example.

SLOW RECOVERY

As women's soccer slowly began to find its feet again, the first women's international game recognized by FIFA was played in 1971, between France and the Netherlands. In 1984 the first UEFA Women's European Championship kicked off, followed by the inaugural FIFA Women's World Cup™ in 1991.

The USA won the first FIFA Women's World Cup™, played in China.

Former USA forward Kristine Lilly (left) has won the most international caps (354) in the history of the sport.

CHANGING THE GAME

Today more than 13 million women and girls play soccer across the globe, with FIFA supporting the growth of women's soccer in all 211 of its member countries. Many women now play professionally, particularly in countries such as the USA, Japan, and across Europe. The game still has a long way to go before pay and conditions match those of the men's game.

REACHING NEW AUDIENCES

As soccer's popularity grew, so did an appetite for the live reporting of the sport. Fans were eager for immediate game updates, which newspapers were unable to offer, unlike radio and television.

RADIO FIRST

On January 22, 1927, the BBC broadcast the first-ever commentary of a league soccer game in England from inside a wooden hut at Highbury Stadium, London. The game was a top-division clash between Arsenal and Sheffield United. Almost a century later, tens of millions of listeners around the world continue to enjoy live radio commentaries of soccer games.

TV COVERAGE

The first full 90-minute game to be aired live on television was an international friendly between England and Scotland in 1938. At the time only around 10,000 people in the United Kingdom owned a television. Sales of television sets rocketed after the Second World War, with televised events such as Queen Elizabeth II's coronation (1953) and the 1948 London Olympics helping to drive demand.

GROWING AUDIENCES

In 1964, the first *Match of the Day* program attracted one quarter of the United Kingdom's adult TV audience, and in 1970 the FA Cup final was broadcast to a record 28 million viewers. The demand for live soccer continued to grow, and in 1992 *Sky Sports* offered more than $500 million to broadcast live games from the newly formed English Premier League (EPL)—a groundbreaking sum of money at the time.

Action from an EPL game in 1992 between Manchester United and Everton.

THE WATCHING WORLD

The first global competition to be aired on TV was the FIFA World Cup Switzerland 1954™. Eight European countries broadcast live games, though they weren't always allocated their home nation. Not all the games were televised and highlights often aired up to three days later. Over the following years, technology improved quickly, and the 1966 tournament acted as a launch pad to reach new audiences around the world.

West Germany celebrate a famous 3–2 victory over favorites Hungary in the final of the FIFA World Cup™ in 1954.

HEADING EAST

Russia hosted the twenty-first edition of the FIFA World Cup™ in 2018. It was the first major FIFA tournament to take place in Eastern Europe and was considered one of the most dramatic and entertaining sports events ever - televised, with more than 3.5 billion viewers worldwide.

In 1970, millions of viewers around the globe watched Pelé's dazzling skills live and in color.

French forward Kylian Mbappé shone at the 2018 FIFA World Cup Russia™, as France became world champions for the second time.

TRUE COLORS

A breakthrough for TV coverage came at the 1970 FIFA World Cup Mexico™ when the games were broadcast in color for the first time. In addition, tens of millions of viewers worldwide were able to watch live games, thanks to advancements in satellite communications. Fans marveled at the color pictures, as Brazil claimed their third title competing in their canary-yellow uniform.

MOST-WATCHED FIFA WORLD CUP™

TOURNAMENT	AUDIENCE (billions)
RUSSIA 2018	3.57
FRANCE 1998	3.4
SOUTH AFRICA 2010	3.2
BRAZIL 2014	3.2
KOREA REP & JAPAN 2002	3

ON THE FIELD

Soccer is the most popular sport on the planet. Two teams, each made up of eleven players, try to score as many goals as possible by kicking or heading a ball into the opposition's net. Games last for ninety minutes and the team that scores the most goals wins.

Belgium's Eden Hazard battles with Phil Jones of England during the FIFA World Cup Russia 2018™ third place play-off game.

FIELD POSITIONS

Soccer is a team sport, with eleven players on each side. The players must each know their role in their team and work together during a game to play at their best.

GOALKEEPER

The only player allowed to handle the ball is the goalkeeper, but only inside their own penalty area. As the team's last line of defense, the keeper has many responsibilities from stopping shots, catching, and throwing the ball, to organizing the defenders. Goalkeepers must stay alert throughout the game, ready to make a save at any moment. Many keepers also start their team's attacking moves from the back, either with a goal kick, pass, or throw.

Italy and AC Milan legend Paolo Maldini is considered to be among the game's greatest defenders.

France's Hugo Lloris makes a diving save during the 2018 FIFA World Cup™.

DEFENDERS

Defenders must try to prevent their opponents from scoring a goal or creating a goalscoring opportunity. While the defenders operate together as a "back line," each has a different role to play. The centerbacks are positioned in front of the goalkeeper and mark the opposition's most attacking forwards. Fullbacks defend the touch line on either side of the field, while wingbacks take up the same position but also join in the attack.

Some teams operate a "sweeper." The sweeper's job is to play behind the defense and improve the passing out to an attacking player.

MIDFIELDERS

The midfield is the link between defense and attack, with players operating in four different midfield roles. Defensive midfielders cover the defense and break up the opposition's attacking play, while central midfielders occupy the middle of the field and look to move the ball forward. Wide midfielders play up and down the touchline providing crosses into the opposition's penalty area, while attacking midfielders try to create goalscoring opportunities.

Midfielder Xavi led Spain to victory at the 2010 FIFA World Cup South Africa™ and to two European titles in 2008 and 2012.

FORWARDS

The main job of a forward is to score goals for the team. As goalscorers they often grab the headlines. A striker, or center forward, plays the furthest forward in the opposition's half. They usually have the most shots on goal and try to hold up the ball to bring others into play. The "second striker" plays in the space between the center forward and the midfield.

Brazil's star forward Marta has been named The Best FIFA Women's Player™ a record six times.

TOP 10 WEARERS

Some of soccer's most iconic players, such as Diego Maradona, Lionel Messi, and Pelé, have sported the No. 10 shirt. The number is commonly worn by the team's playmaker, who controls the team's attacking play and often gets on the score sheet. They must have excellent passing ability, creativity, and vision.

Argentina's Lionel Messi is considered among the world's greatest No. 10s.

UNIQUE SHIRT NUMBERS

JUVENTUS	AC MILAN	AC MILAN	FC INTERNAZIONALE	ABERDEEN

BUFFON 77	SHEVCHENKO 76	RONALDINHO 80	ZAMORANO 1+8	ZEROUALI 0

TEAM FORMATIONS

A formation describes the way a team lines up on the field during a game. The type of formation a team chooses depends on the strengths and weaknesses of the eleven players, both individually and collectively. Here are some of the most common formations in modern soccer.

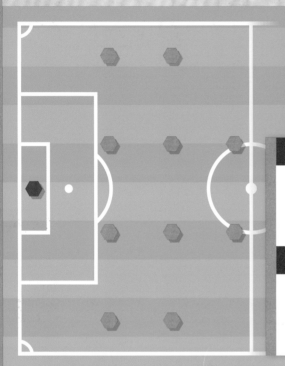

4-4-2

This classic set up is one of the most popular modern formations in soccer. It was commonly used in British football and many parts of Europe throughout the twentieth century.

STRENGTHS

- Two strikers offer a greater attacking threat
- The team can utilize the full width of the field
- Well-defined player roles make the formation easy to implement

WEAKNESSES

- Teams can become outnumbered in midfield
- Midfielders must work extra hard in attack and defense
- Teams are less flexible and passing options are more limited

4-3-3

This formation is effective for teams that have strong attacking players and skillful passers in their line-ups. The formation remains ever popular with some of the world's top teams.

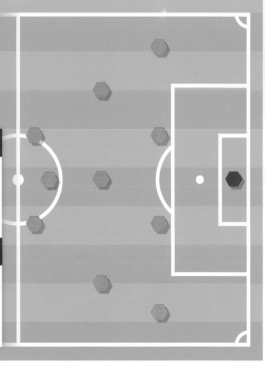

STRENGTHS

- With three players in central positions, teams can control the play
- A congested midfield forces the opposition to play out wide
- Three forwards create more goalscoring opportunities

WEAKNESSES

- Midfielders can often get dragged wide and out of position
- The forwards must be very athletic to provide defensive cover
- Wingbacks must not neglect their defensive duties

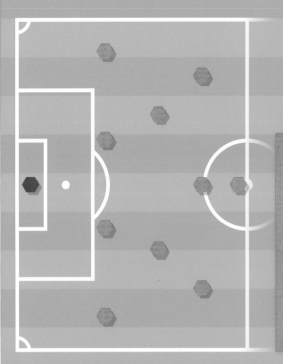

4-2-3-1

Many of the top international and club teams in Europe have employed this formation over the past twenty years. The system utilizes the 4-4-2 diamond's strength in midfield.

STRENGTHS

- It is easy to dominate possession in midfield
- Flexible formation allows players freedom all over the field
- Three attacking midfielders offer teams more creative options

WEAKNESSES

- The lone striker can become isolated if the wide players fail to provide support, forcing the striker to drop back
- Attacking players must play at a high tempo for the whole game

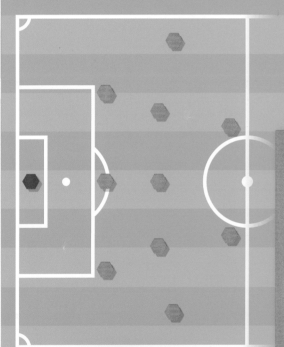

3-5-2

This set-up can adapt to the game situation; it is defensively strong and powerful in attack. With five players in midfield, a team in this formation is likely to dominate possession.

STRENGTHS

- Extra centerback allows a team to foil counterattacks
- Attacking wingbacks provide extra width from the flanks
- Play can be quickly switched from defense to attack

WEAKNESSES

- Centerbacks must have the ball skills to initiate attacks
- Each player must understand their position perfectly
- Wingbacks must have excellent levels of fitness and stamina

Alternative formations include the "diamond" and the "Christmas tree"—so called because of the shape the team forms when its players line up on the field.

THE GAME OFFICIALS

A team of game officials is responsible for a game being played fairly, in line with the Laws of the Game. The referee takes charge, aided by two assistant referees, and a fourth official. In some competitions, video assistant referees help referees make correct decisions —via radio headsets—in major game-changing situations.

THE REFEREE

The referee is essential to the game. They control the game and ensure that it is played fairly and safely. Their main tools are a whistle to interrupt play, a yellow card to caution the player or coach, and a red card to send the person off. They are the final authority for each game that they officiate.

Former soccer referee Pierluigi Collina is widely regarded as one of the best referees of all time.

THE ASSISTANT REFEREE

Two assistant referees help the referee from just outside the touch lines. They mainly concentrate on offside and out of bound situations, but also advise the referee on fouls, especially those that happen close to them. They use their flags to signal substitutions, fouls, offsides, and when the ball goes out of bounds.

THE FOURTH OFFICIAL

The fourth official's main responsibility is to manage the technical areas where the team benches are located. This includes record-keeping and substitutions as well as communicating directly with the coaches as needed. They often show substitutions and added time with electronic boards.

BLAZING A TRAIL

French referee Stéphanie Frappart gave up her playing career at the age of eighteen to follow her dream of becoming a professional game official. Her passion for the Laws of the Game and impressive performances have earned her a reputation as among the top referees in the world.

Women have officiated at two FIFA U-17 World Cups (men's competition). The first was held in India in 2017 and the second hosted by Brazil in 2019.

Frappart made history when she became the first female referee to take charge of a major men's European match, at the 2019 UEFA Super Cup.

VIDEO ASSISTANT REFEREES

A Video Assistant Referee (VAR) and an Assistant VAR (AVAR) review potentially game-changing situations in the Video Operations Room (VOR). They provide the referee with information to correct 'clear and obvious errors' in one of four game-changing situations: goal/no goal, penalty/no penalty, red card, and mistaken identity. Referees have the option to review video clips on a monitor beside the field.

Referee Bastian Dankert signals his intention to review a decision using VAR during a Bundesliga game in 2018.

SOCCER TECHNOLOGY

Technology used in soccer is constantly evolving. Many innovations have been introduced in recent years to improve players' and officials' performance and safety on the field. It is important that any new high-tech idea improves the game without disrupting the flow of the game.

VAR made its debut in a top international tournament at the 2018 FIFA World Cup Russia™.

GOAL-LINE TECHNOLOGY

Goal-line technology (GLT) is used in some of soccer's biggest games, having been introduced following some high-profile incidences at the 2010 FIFA World Cup™. It is a state-of-the-art system that uses cameras—mounted under the stadium roof—to indicate instantly to the referee (via a wrist device) whether or not the whole ball has crossed the goal line. The whole ball must cross the line in order for a goal to be awarded.

VIRTUAL OFFSIDES LINES

Offsides decisions in major competitions are now made with the help of VAR. Virtual lines measure the pinpoint location of players on the field to prove whether or not they were in an offside position when the ball was played to them. The technology was introduced into the Laws of the Game in 2018 and has since proved to be more effective than the naked eye at spotting offside infringements.

VANISHING SPRAY

When a free kick is awarded, the referee uses a special spray to mark out where the defending team must stand (at least 10 yards [9.1m] away from the free kick spot). The foam spray disappears after about a minute.

> The VAR team communicates with the referee only for clear and obvious mistakes or serious missed incidents.

TRACKING DEVICES

Many professional players wear a tracking device during games and training sessions to record key data about their performance. The small sensor, strapped between the player's shoulders, records how far the player has run during a session, their heart rate, and other key fitness information. Teams use this data to assess a player's performance and tailor their training accordingly.

ARTIFICIAL TURF

Although soccer playing surfaces have improved dramatically over the past fifty years, even today games in lower divisions can be postponed due to frozen or waterlogged fields.

Many stadiums now have hybrid fields, which means that artificial fibers have been woven into the natural grass roots. This makes the surface stronger and more resistant to damage.

MODERN STADIUMS

The world's largest soccer stadiums can accommodate more than 100,000 fans. Most modern stadiums are all-seaters that provide fans with a great view of the field. These arenas must also meet the highest safety standards in order to host both sets of fans on game days.

The Lusail Stadium in Qatar is set to have a capacity of 80,000 and will be the largest host stadium at the 2022 FIFA World Cup Qatar™.

THE FIELD

In order to host important competitions, such as the UEFA Champions League or FIFA World Cup™ final, a stadium's field must measure the FIFA standard 115 yards (105m) long by 75 yards (68m) wide. Groundskeepers work diligently to keep the field in perfect condition all year round.

The famous Wembley Stadium hosted Tottenham Hotspur's UEFA Champions League group stage home games during the 2017/18 and 2018/19 seasons.

THE DUGOUT

The coaching staff and substitutes take their seats in the dugout. A technical area is marked out in front of the dugout; the coaches and substitutes are allowed to enter it during a match.

THE DRESSING ROOM

Each team has its own dressing room, where players change into their uniforms and listen to the coach deliver the pregame team talk before taking to the field. Top teams have dressing rooms that include medical beds and ice-bath facilities.

The state-of-the-art home dressing room of premier London team, Tottenham Hotspur.

THE TUNNEL

Players, coaching staff, and mascots line up in the tunnel ready to make their way onto the field. The moments before kick-off can be a nervous time for players.

Players of Italy and Brazil line up in the tunnel at the 2019 FIFA Women's World Cup France™.

LARGEST ALL-SEATER FOOTBALL STADIUMS

RUNGRADO 1ST OF MAY STADIUM
TEAM: Korea DPR
CAPACITY: 114,000
LOCATION: Pyongyang, Korea DPR

MELBOURNE CRICKET GROUND
TEAM: Australia
CAPACITY: 100,024
LOCATION: Melbourne, Australia

CAMP NOU
TEAM: FC Barcelona
CAPACITY: 99,354
LOCATION: Barcelona, Spain

FNB STADIUM (SOCCER CITY)
TEAMS: Kaizer Chiefs, South Africa
CAPACITY: 94,736
LOCATION: Johannesburg, South Africa

ROSE BOWL STADIUM
TEAM: UCLA Bruins
CAPACITY: 90,888
LOCATION: Pasadena, California, USA

WEMBLEY STADIUM
TEAMS: England (Men's & Women's National)
CAPACITY: 90,000
LOCATION: London, England

ESTADIO AZTECA
TEAMS: Club América, Cruz Azul
CAPACITY: 87,523
LOCATION: Mexico City, Mexico

BUKIT JALIL NATIONAL STADIUM
TEAMS: Malaysia
CAPACITY: 87,411
LOCATION: Kuala Lumpur, Malaysia

BORG EL ARAB STADIUM
TEAMS: Egypt
CAPACITY: 86,000
LOCATION: Alexandria, Egypt

MAJOR TOURNAMENTS

Some of the most famous prizes in the game are won at international tournaments. Every player dreams of one day lifting world soccer's top trophy for their country, the FIFA World Cup Trophy. Each country also has the opportunity to be crowned champion of its continent in a number of exciting knockout tournaments played around the globe.

Cesc Fàbregas lifts the trophy after Spain win the 2010 FIFA World Cup South Africa™ by defeating the Netherlands 1–0 in the final.

FIFA WORLD CUP™

The FIFA World Cup™ is the most prestigious competition in world soccer. The men's tournament takes place every four years to decide which national team will be crowned world champions.

France were crowned world champions after winning the 2018 FIFA World Cup Russia™.

CURRENT CHAMPIONS

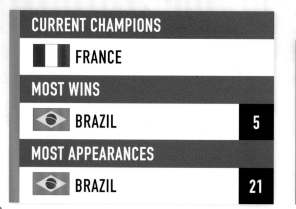
FRANCE

MOST WINS
BRAZIL — 5

MOST APPEARANCES
BRAZIL — 21

TOURNAMENT FACTS

WORLD CUP	YEAR	HOST NATION		NO. OF TEAMS
FIRST EDITION	1930	URUGUAY		13
LATEST EDITION	2018	RUSSIA		32
NEXT EDITION	2022	QATAR		32

32 THE FINAL PHASE

Currently the final phase of the FIFA World Cup™ is played by thirty-two teams. While the host nation(s) and reigning champions automatically receive a place, the remaining teams from the six confederations play a series of qualifying games in the three years leading up to the event.

A record-breaking **3.5 billion people**—almost half of the world's population—tuned in to watch at least one game during the 2018 FIFA World Cup Russia™.

25 GERMAN GREAT

Legendary German captain Lothar Matthäus holds the record for the most appearances (twenty-five) in the final phases of the FIFA World Cup™.

17 HISTORY MAKER

Northern Ireland's Norman Whiteside is the youngest player to feature in the FIFA World Cup™ final phase. He was just seventeen years and forty-one days old when he lined up against Yugoslavia in 1982.

2 DOUBLE WINNER

Italy's Vittorio Pozzo is the only coach to have won the FIFA World Cup™ twice. He led the *Azzurri* to back-to-back victories in 1934 and 1938.

TOURNAMENT AWARDS

At the end of each tournament, trophies are awarded to players for their outstanding performances. In addition, the team with the fewest red and yellow cards wins a fair play prize.

- ⚽ ADIDAS GOLDEN BALL AWARD—best player
- ⚽ ADIDAS GOLDEN BOOT AWARD—top goalscorer
- ⚽ ADIDAS GOLDEN GLOVE AWARD—best goalkeeper
- ⚽ BEST YOUNG PLAYER AWARD—best player under twenty-one at the start of the calendar year
- ⚽ FIFA FAIR PLAY TROPHY—team with the best record of fair play (only teams who reach the knockout stages qualify for consideration)

Croatia's Luka Modrić claimed the adidas Golden Ball at the 2018 FIFA World Cup Russia™, while France's Kylian Mbappé won the FIFA Best Young Player Award.

Colombia forward James Rodríguez scored six goals at the 2018 FIFA World Cup Brazil™ to clinch the adidas Golden Boot Award.

LEADING LEGENDS

Brazil are the most successful team in FIFA World Cup™ history. The South American side have won five FIFA World Cup™ titles and have played at an unrivaled twenty-one tournaments. Their famous forward Pelé wore the No. 10 shirt, winning three FIFA World Cup™ tournaments with Brazil in 1958, 1962, and 1970. He is regarded among the greatest players that soccer has ever produced.

Pelé scored 12 goals in 14 FIFA World Cup™ appearances.

TOP PRIZE

The FIFA World Cup™ Trophy is 14.5 inches tall, weighs 13.6 pounds and is made of 18-carat gold. After each tournament the winning team's name is engraved on the trophy's base. The previous prize, called the Jules Rimet Cup, disappeared in 1966 and was later found by a dog called Pickles. In 1983, the cup vanished again in Brazil.

ALL-TIME TOURNAMENT TOP GOALSCORERS

PLAYER		GOALS	YEARS
MIROSLAV KLOSE		16	2002, 2006, 2010, 2014
RONALDO		15	1998, 2002, 2006
GERD MÜLLER		14	1970, 1974
JUST FONTAINE		13	1958
PELÉ		12	1958, 1962, 1966, 1970

Germany's Miroslav Klose scored a record 16 goals across four World Cup tournaments. He had a grand goal celebration, too.

FORTHCOMING COMPETITION

Qatar has been chosen to host the 2022 FIFA World Cup™. It will be the first time that the tournament is being held in the Middle East. In order to avoid Qatar's searing summer heat, the tournament will kick off in winter for the first time. The final is set to be played at the 80,000-seater Lusail national stadium, the construction of which started in 2017 and is due to be completed in time to stage the tournament.

The final of the 1999 FIFA Women's World Cup USA™ attracted 90,185 fans—a women's record.

TOP TEN FIFA WORLD CUP™ ATTENDANCES

1 🇧🇷 173,850
Estadio do Maracanã
Rio de Janeiro,
Brazil 1950

2 🇲🇽 114,600
Estadio Azteca
Mexico City, Mexico 1986

3 🇲🇽 107,412
Estadio Azteca
Mexico City, Mexico 1970

4 98,000
Wembley Stadium
London, England 1966

5 🇺🇸 94,194
Rose Bowl
Pasadena, USA 1994

6 🇺🇾 93,000
Estadio Centenario
Montevideo,
Uruguay 1930

7 90,000
Estadio Santiago Bernabéu
Madrid, Spain 1982

8 🇿🇦 84,490
Soccer City
Johannesburg,
South Africa 2010

9 80,000
Stade de France
Paris, France 1998

10 78,011
Luzhniki Stadium
Moscow, Russia 2018

FIFA WOMEN'S WORLD CUP™

The first FIFA Women's World Cup™ was played in China in 1991. Since then, the tournament has grown to become one of the greatest sporting competitions for women on the planet.

The number of viewers watching the FIFA Women's World Cup™ globally passed **1 billion people** for the first time in 2019—82 million people watched the final between the USA and the Netherlands.

The USA has a fantastic record in the competition, claiming a total of four titles from eight tournaments.

CURRENT CHAMPIONS

 USA

MOST WINS

USA | 4

MOST APPEARANCES

		=8
 BRAZIL		
GERMANY		
JAPAN		
NIGERIA		
NORWAY		
SWEDEN		
USA		

TOURNAMENT FACTS

WOMEN'S WORLD CUP	YEAR	HOST NATION	NO. OF TEAMS
FIRST EDITION	1991	CHINA PR	12
LATEST EDITION	2019	FRANCE	24
NEXT EDITION	2023	AUS/N ZEALAND	32

LEADING LADIES

The USA are the most successful team at the FIFA Women's World Cup™, winning the trophy a record four times. Their first title came at the inaugural edition in China PR in 1991, where they beat Norway 2–1 in the final.

8 MOST RECENT EDITION

The 2019 FIFA Women's World Cup™ in France was the eighth time the tournament has been played. Prior to that, unofficial international tournaments took place in 1970 and 1971, at a time when several countries around the world had just lifted their bans on women's soccer. FIFA held the first official Women's World Cup™ in 1991 in China, with the tournament featuring twelve teams.

16 YOUNG SHOULDERS

Ifeanyi Chiejine is the youngest woman to have played at a FIFA Women's World Cup™. She was sixteen years and thirty-four days when she played for Nigeria in 1999.

17 GOLDEN GIRL

Brazil's Marta has scored more FIFA World Cup goals than any other player, male or female. She has netted a record seventeen goals over five tournaments.

2 DOUBLE WINNER

Jill Ellis is the only manager to have led her team to glory at the FIFA Women's World Cup™ twice. She won back-to-back titles with the USA in 2015 and 2019.

32 GLOBAL GAME

Teams from the six confederations (see p.12–13) around the world will try to claim one of thirty-two places at the biggest ever FIFA Women's World Cup™ in 2023. Last time twenty-four teams were featured.

7 FANTASTIC FORMIGA

Formiga is another Brazilian record-breaker. The midfielder has represented Brazil in the final phase of seven FIFA Women's World Cups™.

ALL-TIME TOURNAMENT TOP GOALSCORERS

PLAYER		GOALS	YEARS
MARTA	🇧🇷	17	2003, 2007, 2011, 2015, 2019
BIRGIT PRINZ		14	1995, 1999, 2003, 2007, 2011
ABBY WAMBACH	🇺🇸	14	2003, 2007, 2011, 2015
MICHELLE AKERS	🇺🇸	12	1991, 1995, 1999
CRISTIANE	🇧🇷	11	2003, 2007, 2011, 2015, 2019
SUN WEN	🇨🇳	11	1991, 1995, 1999, 2003
BETTINA WIEGMANN		11	1991, 1995, 1999, 2003

OLYMPIC GAMES (MEN'S TOURNAMENT)

Men's soccer first featured at the summer Olympic Games in 1900, although the competition was not recognized by FIFA as an official tournament until the 1908 Games in London. The race to qualify is fierce; there are just sixteen spots for teams from around the world to fill.

Brazil salute the crowd after winning the gold medal in the men's soccer competition at the 2016 Games.

CURRENT CHAMPIONS

🇧🇷 BRAZIL

MOST WINS

HUNGARY | 3
GREAT BRITAIN

MOST APPEARANCES

ITALY | 14

YOUNG TALENT

Until 1984, only amateur players were allowed to compete in the tournament. Professionals may now play, but squads must comprise mainly of players who are under twenty-three. Stars such as Lionel Messi and Sergio Agüero (below) made a name for themselves on the world stage at the Olympic Games.

*Event postponed until 2021 following the global outbreak of the COVID-19 virus in 2020.

TOURNAMENT FACTS

OLYMPIC GAMES	YEAR	HOST NATION		NATIONS
FIRST EDITION	1900	FRANCE		3
LATEST EDITION	2016	BRAZIL		16
NEXT EDITION	2021*	JAPAN		16

64 BRAZIL MAKE HISTORY

In 1952, after their first appearance at an Olympic Games in 64 years, Brazil finally struck gold when they hosted the Games in 2016. In the final match versus Germany, Neymar Jr. scored the winning spot kick in a penalty shoot-out to write Brazil's name in the history books at last.

LAST TEN GOLD MEDALISTS

HOST CITY	YEAR	WINNER
RIO	2016	BRAZIL
LONDON	2012	MEXICO
BEIJING	2008	ARGENTINA
ATHENS	2004	ARGENTINA
SYDNEY	2000	CAMEROON
ATLANTA	1996	NIGERIA
BARCELONA	1992	SPAIN
SEOUL	1988	USSR
LOS ANGELES	1984	FRANCE
MOSCOW	1980	CZECHOSLOVAKIA

13 SHARP SHOOTER

Denmark's Sophus Nielsen has scored the most goals in men's Olympic history with a not-so-unlucky thirteen strikes (1908 and 1912 Games).

Lionel Messi (right) led Argentina to their second gold medal in a row after an undefeated run at the Olympic Games in 2008.

3 GOLD STANDARD

Winners of a hat-trick of gold medals in 1952, 1964, and 1968, Hungary are known as the "Golden Team" in Olympic soccer. They dazzled at the tournament in 1952 when they were led by their legendary captain Ferenc Puskás (left).

2 AFRICAN ACES

Nigeria and Cameroon are the only two African Olympic gold medalists. Nigeria beat Argentina 3–2 at the 1996 Games and Cameroon beat Spain in a penalty shoot-out at the 2000 Games in Sydney.

OLYMPIC GAMES (WOMEN'S TOURNAMENT)

Introduced in 1996, the women's tournament has since grown into a popular Olympic event. With no age restrictions, the world's finest female players usually feature at the Games.

GOLDEN GIRLS OF AMERICA

Having won four of the last six women's soccer tournaments at the Olympic Games, the USA have set the gold standard. At the 2012 Games in London, they faced Japan, who had previously beaten them on penalties in the final of the 2011 FIFA Women's World Cup™. Two goals from Carli Lloyd earned the USA a record fourth Olympic gold medal in front of 80,000 people at a packed Wembley Stadium.

CURRENT CHAMPIONS

GERMANY

MOST WINS

USA — 4

MOST APPEARANCES

BRAZIL — 6

SWEDEN

USA

TOURNAMENT FACTS

*Event postponed until 2021 following the global outbreak of the COVID-19 virus in 2020.

OLYMPIC GAMES	YEAR	HOST NATION		NO. OF TEAMS
FIRST EDITION	1996	USA		8
LATEST EDITION	2016	BRAZIL		12
NEXT EDITION	2021*	JAPAN		12

14 FOLLOW THE LEADER

Brazil's Cristiane (right) is the leading scorer in the competition with fourteen goals, scored over four Olympic Games (2004, 2008, 2012, and 2016).

GOLD MEDALISTS

OLYMPIC GAMES	YEAR	CHAMPIONS
RIO	2016	GERMANY
LONDON	2012	USA
BEIJING	2008	USA
ATHENS	2004	USA
SYDNEY	2000	NORWAY
ATLANTA	1996	USA

6 LIVING LEGEND

In addition to her FIFA Women's World Cup™ feats, Brazil midfielder Formiga has also played in a record six Olympic Games, between 1996 and 2016.

2 EUROPE'S BEST

Only two teams from Europe, Norway and Germany, have won Olympic gold so far. Sweden have won a silver medal, while Germany have also secured the bronze medal three times.

71 GOAL FEAST

Women's soccer at the 2012 Games provided a festival of goals, with a total of seventy-one strikes hitting the back of the net—a record total at an Olympic Games.

2 SUPER SWEDE

Swede Pia Sundhage is the only coach to have won two Olympic gold medals, leading the USA to victory twice. A legendary player herself for Sweden, Pia now manages Brazil.

TEAM GB

While teams from England, Wales, Scotland, and Northern Ireland play as separate countries in other international tournaments, these nations competed as Great Britain at their first Olympic Games in 2012. The team reached the quarter-finals, eventually losing to Canada. Team GB will make its second appearance at the Tokyo Games in 2021*.

UEFA EUROPEAN CHAMPIONSHIP

Known more commonly as the EUROs, this tournament offers European teams the chance to prove themselves as the top nation on the continent. The UEFA European Championship is ordinarily held every four years and has grown from four teams to twenty-four top European teams.

CUP RETURNS TO ROME

Captained by Giorgio Chiellini (right), Italy triumphed at the UEFA EURO 2020 to win the trophy for the second time in their history. In the final, they played England in London's Wembley Stadium. With the match tied at 1–1 after extra time, Italy beat the home side 3–2 on penalties.

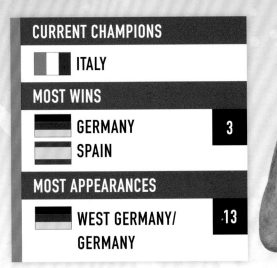

CURRENT CHAMPIONS

	ITALY

MOST WINS

GERMANY	3
SPAIN	

MOST APPEARANCES

WEST GERMANY/ GERMANY	13

*Event moved to 2021 following the global outbreak of the COVID-19 virus in 2020.

TOURNAMENT FACTS

EUROS	YEAR	HOST NATION		NO. OF TEAMS
FIRST EDITION	1960	FRANCE		4
LATEST EDITION	2021*	EUROPE		24
NEXT EDITION	2024	GERMANY		24

A EUROPEAN CELEBRATION

The sixteenth edition of the tournament was delayed a year as a result of the global outbreak of COVID-19. Eleven nations jointly hosted the tournament in 2021 as fans were invited to celebrate 60 years since the first European Championship took place. London's Wembley Stadium staged the final between Italy and England.

14 GOAL KING

Cristiano Ronaldo is the top scorer in the tournament's history, with 14 goals in five competitions. He has also netted a record 31 goals in qualifying matches.

67 EARLY GOAL

The fastest-ever strike came at UEFA EURO 2004, when Russia's Dmitri Kirichenko scored after 67 seconds against Greece.

10 PERFECT TEN

Ten different countries have won the famous Henri Delaunay Cup so far, with just two nations from Eastern Europe—the former Soviet Union in 1960 and Czechoslovakia in 1976—among the winners.

1 EURO HEROES

Greece (below) pulled off a major shock when they beat hosts Portugal to win their first-ever (and so far only) trophy at the UEFA EURO 2004. A single strike in the final by Angelos Charisteas was enough to etch Greece's name on the trophy forever.

UEFA WOMEN'S EUROPEAN CHAMPIONSHIP

The Women's edition of the UEFA European Championship kicked off in 1984. The competition was originally held biennially and contested by just four teams, Sixteen nations qualify for the modern tournament, held every four years since 1997.

HOME WIN

The Netherlands (below) won their first Women's European Championship when they hosted the tournament in 2017. After beating Denmark 4–2 in the final, their fans painted the town orange. Over half of the country watched the final on television, as the popularity of women's soccer exploded in the Netherlands and players became celebrities following their triumph.

CURRENT CHAMPIONS

 NETHERLANDS	

MOST WINS

WEST GERMANY/ GERMANY	8

MOST APPEARANCES

ITALY	11
NORWAY	

TOURNAMENT FACTS

*Event moved from 2021 to 2022 following the global outbreak of the COVID-19 virus in 2020.

WOMEN'S EURO	YEAR	HOST NATION		NO. OF TEAMS
FIRST EDITION	1984	EUROPE		4
LATEST EDITION	2017	NETHERLANDS		16
NEXT EDITION	2022*	ENGLAND		16

UEFA Women's EURO 2017 hosts, the Netherlands, sold out all their games in the tournament. The six games were watched by a total of 110,897 spectators.

UEFA WOMEN'S EURO TOP SCORERS

PLAYER		GOALS	YEAR
JODIE TAYLOR		5	2017
LOTTA SCHELIN		5	2013
INKA GRINGS		6	2009
INKA GRINGS		4	2005
CLAUDIA MÜLLER		3	2001
SANDRA SMISEK		3	2001

GERMANY'S GLORY

Crowned European champions eight times, Germany have been incredible at the UEFA Women's European Championship. They won the competition six times in a row between 1995 and 2013, with their most recent victory coming in 2013. They've played the most games (40) and recorded the most wins, too (31).

5 FIVE-TIMERS

German forward Birgit Prinz won five UEFA Women's EURO titles during Germany's golden age. Goalkeeper Nadine Angerer holds the same record, although she was an unused substitute in three of these wins.

4 FAB FOUR

Four different nations have won the title since the tournament began—Germany, Norway, Sweden, and the Netherlands.

75 GOALS GALORE

UEFA Women's EURO 2009 in Finland was a spectacle for fans, as together the teams chalked up seventy-five goals—the most goals scored in any EURO tournament.

18 TRIPLE SCORE

Sweden's Lena Videkull took just eighteen minutes to score the fastest hat-trick in the tournament's history in 1995 against neighbors Norway.

CONMEBOL COPA AMÉRICA

The *Copa América* is the biggest international tournament in South America. It is the oldest competition played between international teams in world soccer and was first held in 1916.

More than 148,000 spectators watched Brazil beat Uruguay in the 1989 tournament decider in Rio de Janeiro. Today, the Maracanã Stadium "only" holds about 79,000 fans.

Argentina celebrate victory over hosts Brazil in the *Copa América* 2021 final Rio's Maracanã Stadium.

CURRENT CHAMPIONS

ARGENTINA	

MOST WINS

URUGUAY	
ARGENTINA	15

MOST APPEARANCES

URUGUAY	44

TOURNAMENT FACTS

*Likely destination but not formally decided at the time of print.

COPA AMÉRICA	YEAR	HOST NATION		NO. OF TEAMS
FIRST EDITION	1916	ARGENTINA		4
LATEST EDITION	2021	BRAZIL		10
NEXT EDITION	2024	ECUADOR*		10

3 TRIPLE MISS

In 1999, Argentine striker Martin Palermo earned an unwanted place in soccer folklore (and the *Guinness Book of World Records*). He missed three penalties in a single game, in a group competition against Colombia.

2001 FAMOUS WIN

When Honduras replaced Argentina at the 2001 *Copa América* in Colombia, their small squad arrived in the country just hours before their first match kicked off. A shock win against Brazil in the quarter-finals saw Honduras secure a historic victory, as the minnows went on to finish third.

17 COPA KINGS

Argentina's Norberto Méndez and Brazil's Zizinho are *Copa América's* all-time leading scorers, with both players tied at seventeen goals each.

COPA AMÉRICA FEMENINA

Founded in 1991, the *Copa América Femenina* offers women's teams the chance to become champions of South America. Just three nations (Brazil, Chile, and Venezuela) played in the first tournament. Now ten teams contest the cup every four years.

7 WONDER WOMEN

Brazil have dominated the cup, winning the title seven times out of eight since the tournament was first hosted. Argentina are the only other winner, having claimed victory in 2006.

16 UNSTOPPABLE

Brazil's Roseli hit an unbeaten scoring streak at the 1998 *Copa América Femenina*. Her sixteen goals in six games is a record that may never be broken.

A strong performance in the *Copa América Femenina* allows teams to qualify for the FIFA Women's World Cup™ and the Olympic Games.

Two goals from Mônica (left, center) in the final secured Brazil's win at the 2019 *Copa América Femenina*.

CONCACAF GOLD CUP

Held biennially, the Concacaf Gold Cup (known as the Concacaf Championship from 1963 to 1989) is the biggest international tournament for North America, Central America, and the Caribbean region. As of 2019, sixteen teams qualify for the competition.

Mexico celebrate after beating the USA to win the 2019 Concacaf Gold Cup for a record eighth time.

FIERCE RIVALS

Concacaf's greatest rivalry is between the two titans, Mexico and the USA. Mexico have won eight Gold Cups, while the USA have secured the prize an impressive six times. The two teams clashed most recently in the final of the 2019 competition, in which a single strike from Jonathan dos Santos (far right) blasted Mexico to glory.

CURRENT CHAMPIONS

MEXICO

MOST WINS

MEXICO	
GOLD CUP	8
CONCACAF CHAMPIONSHIP	3

MOST APPEARANCES

MEXICO	23

TOURNAMENT FACTS

CONCACAF	YEAR	HOST NATION		NO. OF TEAMS
FIRST EDITION	1963	EL SALVADOR		9
LATEST EDITION	2019	USA		16
		COSTA RICA		
		JAMAICA		
NEXT EDITION	2021	USA		16

3 BEST BOSSES

Former USA head coach Bruce Arena claimed a record third Concacaf Gold Cup in 2017. Former Serbian international Bora Milutinović is the only coach to have won the cup with two different teams—the USA in 1991 and Mexico in 1996.

2015 REGGAE BOYZ

Jamaica made history in 2015 when they became the first Caribbean nation to reach the Gold Cup final. A shock victory against the USA in the quarter-finals won the Jamaicans many new fans, despite Mexico ultimately claiming the title.

18 GOAL GETTER

USA forward Landon Donovan netted a record eighteen goals in the Concacaf Gold Cup, playing for the Stars and Stripes between 2000 and 2014.

CONCACAF WOMEN'S CHAMPIONSHIP

The top prize for women's international teams in the region is the Concacaf Women's Championship. Many CWC tournaments have served as a pathway for teams to qualify for the FIFA Women's World Cup™.

1991 KICKING OFF

Haiti hosted the first CWC almost three decades ago. The winners were the USA, who powered five goals past Canada in the final.

8 STANDING OUT

No team comes close to matching the USA's record in the competition. They've won the championship a record eight times, while Canada are second best with two trophies.

5 CANADA'S CURSE

Canada have finished as tournament runners-up five times, coming closest to winning the CWC in 2006 and 2002, when they lost to a golden goal in extra time.

Teammates Alex Morgan and Carli Lloyd celebrate the USA's winning goal against Canada in 2018.

AFRICA CUP OF NATIONS

The Africa Cup of Nations (AFCON) has a rich history, dating back to 1957. The first tournament featured just Ethiopia, Sudan, and Egypt. The competition is now staged every two years, and twenty-four African nations take part.

South Africa claimed the trophy in their very first appearance in the AFCON, in 1996. Their famous president, Nelson Mandela (center), joined the historic celebrations.

From 2013, the Africa Cup of Nations was switched to being held in odd-numbered years to avoid clashing with the FIFA World Cup™.

CURRENT CHAMPIONS

ALGERIA

MOST WINS

EGYPT — 7

MOST APPEARANCES

EGYPT — 24

TOURNAMENT FACTS

*Event moved from 2021 to 2022 following the global outbreak of the COVID-19 virus in 2020.

AFCON	YEAR	HOST NATION		NO. OF TEAMS
FIRST EDITION	1957	SUDAN		3
LATEST EDITION	2019	EGYPT		24
NEXT EDITION	2022*	CAMEROON		24

CAMEROON'S LION

Samuel Eto'o is considered to be among the best players ever to have appeared in the competition. His performances for Cameroon saw him score an unbeaten eighteen goals in six different contests of the tournament. Eto'o was an AFCON winner with Cameroon twice—in 2000 and 2002.

11–10
MEMORABLE MATCH

The 1992 final between Ivory Coast and Ghana was a nail-biting affair that went to a penalty shoot-out. Ivory Coast went on to win the shoot-out 11–10 to claim their first trophy. It was the first time in a game that every player on the field took a penalty kick in a major international final.

7 EGYPTIAN KINGS

Egypt's win in 2010 saw them extend their lead at the top of the AFCON champions table. Their victory over Ghana in the final was the seventh time they had won the competition and a record third crown in a row.

75,000
UNEXPECTED SUCCESS

Algeria became champions for only the second time in their history when they beat Senegal in 2019. They held on to an early lead to take the trophy (below) in front of 75,000 fans at the Cairo International Stadium, Egypt.

9 MULAMBA RECORD

At the 1974 edition, Zaire's Ndaye Mulamba found the net nine times. It is the highest number of goals scored by one player in a single AFCON tournament.

8 WOMEN'S EDITION

Eight nations compete in the Africa Women Cup of Nations, which was first held in 1991. Nigeria are the top women's team with eleven trophies, while their midfielder Perpetua Nkwocha (right) has been the tournament's top scorer on four occasions.

AFC ASIAN CUP

The AFC Asian Cup is the world's second oldest international soccer championship. The first competition took place in Hong Kong in 1956, featuring just four teams in the final phase. Nine different nations have since won the trophy.

Qatar celebrate their first-ever triumph in the competition after beating Japan in 2019.

CURRENT CHAMPIONS	
QATAR	
MOST WINS	
JAPAN	4
MOST APPEARANCES	
IRAN	14
KOREA REPUBLIC	

TOURNAMENT FACTS

AFC ASIAN CUP	YEAR	HOST NATION	NO. OF TEAMS
FIRST EDITION	1956	BRITISH HONG KONG	4
LATEST EDITION	2019	UNITED ARAB EMIRATES	24
NEXT EDITION	2023	CHINA PR	24

14 DAZZLING DAEI

No player has scored more AFC Asian Cup goals than Iran's Ali Daei (right). His goal-scoring record stands at fourteen.

9 PROLIFIC ALI

Qatar's Almoez Ali netted nine goals at the AFC Asian Cup in 2019. He holds the record for the most goals scored in a single AFC Asian Cup year.

Australia switched confederations from the OFC to the AFC in 2006. Now both their men's and women's teams can qualify to play in the AFC Asian Cup. Their women's team were first crowned AFC champions in 2010, and the men's team won the tournament in 2015.

AFC WOMEN'S ASIAN CUP

Featuring twelve teams (from 2022), the AFC Women's Asian Cup is the premier women's soccer competition in Asia. Japan are the current champions, having won the title in 2018.

Japan's players celebrate with the trophy after winning the AFC Women's Asian Cup final game against Australia in 2018.

16 AUSSIE RULES

Australia's women claimed their first Asian Cup just four years after joining the AFC. Sixteen-year-old striker Sam Kerr scored first, but Korea DPR equalized to take the game to extra time and penalties. Australia won the shoot-out 5–4.

8 FAR EAST DOMINANCE

The competition has been dominated by countries from the Pacific Rim, with China PR's women's national soccer team having won eight times, including a series of seven back-to-back victories.

60 GAME TIME

From 1975 to 1981, AFC Women's Asian Cup games were only 60 minutes long. Since 2014, the competition has served as a qualifying tournament for the FIFA Women's World Cup™.

TOP NATIONS IN SOCCER

Soccer is a truly global sport and FIFA, representing 211 member associations, is the main governing body. Many of the most memorable games are played on the international stage, where the world's most famous soccer nations compete for the glory of winning the biggest trophies in the game.

Philipp Lahm lifts the trophy in celebration after Germany defeat Argentina 1–0 in the 2014 FIFA World Cup Brazil™ final.

ENGLAND (MEN'S)

England played its first official international game in 1872 in Partick, Scotland. Nicknamed *The Three Lions*, England's sole victory at a major tournament came in 1966, when they won the FIFA World Cup™ on home turf.

England lineup ahead of their 2018 FIFA World Cup Russia™ third-place playoff against Belgium.

So far, 143 clubs have contributed players to the England team. North London team Tottenham Hotspur have provided the most with 78.

TEAM FACTS

JOINED FIFA: 1905	
HIGHEST FIFA/COCA-COLA WORLD RANKING: 1	
STADIUM: Wembley Stadium (London)	
HONORS: FIFA World Cup 1966 (winners)	
FIFA WORLD CUP™ APPEARANCES: 15	
UEFA EUROPEAN CHAMPIONSHIP APPEARANCES: 9	

TOP SCORERS

1. WAYNE ROONEY	53
2. BOBBY CHARLTON	49
3. GARY LINEKER	48
4. JIMMY GREAVES	44
5. MICHAEL OWEN	40

HISTORY BOYS

England famously won the FIFA World Cup™ final in 1966. Played at Wembley Stadium, Geoff Hurst became the only man to score a hat-trick in a FIFA World Cup™ final, as England beat West Germany 4–2 after extra time. Captain Bobby Moore lifted the Jules Rimet Trophy to the delight of the home crowd.

LEADING LION

Striker Gary Lineker holds the England record for the most goals scored at the FIFA World Cup™ with ten strikes across the 1986 and 1990 tournaments. His goal-poaching instinct saw him claim the adidas Golden Boot at the 1986 FIFA World Cup Mexico™, with six goals.

ROONEY'S RECORDS

Striker Wayne Rooney enjoyed an impressive England career. He is the leading scorer with 53 goals, as well as the country's youngest goalscorer, scoring when he was just seventeen years and 317 days old. Rooney made the most appearances of any outfield player before retiring from international soccer in 2018.

MOST APPEARANCES

#	Player	Appearances
1.	PETER SHILTON	125
2.	WAYNE ROONEY	120
3.	DAVID BECKHAM	115
4.	STEVEN GERRARD	114
5.	BOBBY MOORE	108

ENGLAND (WOMEN'S)

The Lionesses qualified for their first UEFA Women's European Championship in 1984, finishing as runners-up. England have since become a top side in the world and have appeared at the final phase of the FIFA Women's World Cup™ five times,

The first official women's soccer game in England took place on March 23 1985. The North beat the South 7–1.

The England lineup before their semifinal game against the USA at the 2019 FIFA Women's World Cup™.

TEAM FACTS

HIGHEST FIFA/COCA-COLA WOMEN'S WORLD RANKING: 2	
HONORS: FIFA Women's World Cup 2015 (third place); UEFA Women's Championship (runners-up) 1984, 2009	
FIFA WOMEN'S WORLD CUP™ APPEARANCES: 5	
UEFA WOMEN'S CHAMPIONSHIP APPEARANCES: 8	
OLYMPIC GAMES APPEARANCES: 1 (as part of Team GB)	

TOP SCORERS

1.	KELLY SMITH	46
2.	KERRY DAVIS	44
3.	KAREN WALKER	40
=	FARA WILLIAMS	
5.	ELLEN WHITE	39

MOST APPEARANCES

1.	FARA WILLIAMS	172
2.	JILL SCOTT	151
3.	KAREN CARNEY	144
4.	ALEX SCOTT	140
5.	CASEY STONEY	130

FABULOUS FARA

England's most-capped player of all time, midfielder Fara Williams (left), made her debut for England at seventeen in an international career that spanned two decades. Williams will be remembered for scoring the winning penalty as England defeated Germany for the first time to finish third at the 2015 FIFA Women's World Cup™ in Canada.

BRONZE AWARDS

Defender Lucy Bronze won the adidas Silver Ball award at the 2019 FIFA Women's World Cup France™ as the second most outstanding player at the tournament. In 2020 she won the Best FIFA Women's award. The England vice-captain is known for her surging runs and spectacular volleyed goals. She has won more than eighty caps for her country.

SCORING SENSATION

Forward Kelly Smith is considered among the most technically gifted players ever to play for England. With 117 caps, Kelly remains England's record scorer with forty-six goals. She appeared in two FIFA Women's World Cup™ tournaments, three UEFA Women's Championships, and also took part at the 2012 Olympic Games in London, as part of Team GB.

FRANCE (MEN'S)

Current FIFA World Cup™ holders and two-time world champions, France boast a rich history. Created in 1904, *Les Bleus* (The Blues) have qualified for the FIFA World Cup™ fifteen times and have played in the UEFA European Championship ten times.

France celebrate winning the FIFA World Cup™ trophy for a second time in 2018.

Goalkeeper Fabien Barthez has made the most FIFA World Cup™ appearances of any male player for France—17 from 1998 to 2006.

TEAM FACTS

JOINED FIFA: 1907

HIGHEST FIFA/COCA-COLA WORLD RANKING: 1

STADIUM: Stade de France (Paris)

HONORS: FIFA World Cup 1998, 2018 (winners); UEFA European Championship 1984, 2000 (winners); Olympic Games 1984 (gold medal), 1900 (silver medal)

FIFA WORLD CUP™ APPEARANCES: 15

UEFA EUROPEAN CHAMPIONSHIP APPEARANCES: 9

TOP SCORERS

1. THIERRY HENRY	51	
2. OLIVIER GIROUD	46	
3. MICHEL PLATINI	41	
4. DAVID TREZEGUET	34	
5. ANTOINE GRIEZMANN	38	

KING HENRY

The great Thierry Henry (right) struck fifty-one times for France and broke Michel Platini's scoring record for the national team in 2007. The forward is the only Frenchman to play at the FIFA World Cup™ four times, helping France to win in 1998. He was also a key member of the squad that helped *Les Bleus* to glory at the UEFA EURO 2000.

The world-famous training complex, Clairefontaine National Football Institute, has produced many of France's top players.

GOAL HERO

Striker Just Fontaine (left) holds the record for the most goals scored at a single FIFA World Cup™ —thirteen in six games in 1958. He remains the only Frenchman to have scored a hat-trick at the tournament, and he was even head coach for the national side for two games in 1967.

TEEN TITAN

Forward Kylian Mbappé helped France win their second FIFA World Cup™ in 2018, scoring a goal in the final as a nineteen year old. The only other teenager to have scored in the final of a FIFA World Cup™ is Pelé. At the 2018 edition. Kylian Mbappé became France's youngest goalscorer at a major tournament.

MOST APPEARANCES

1. LILIAN THURAM	142
2. HUGO LLORIS	129
3. THIERRY HENRY	123
4. MARCEL DESAILLY	116
5. OLIVIER GIROUD	110

FRANCE (WOMEN'S)

Although a women's national league was created in 1974, *Les Bleues* (The Blues) played a number of times but did not qualify for a UEFA European Championship tournament until 1997. They made their first FIFA Women's World Cup™ appearance in 2003.

France's top lscorer at the FIFA Women's World Cup 2019™ was a defender! Centerback Wendie Renard scored four times in the competition.

France lost to eventual champions the USA at the 2019 FIFA Women's World Cup™.

TEAM FACTS

HIGHEST FIFA/COCA-COLA WOMEN'S WORLD RANKING: 3

HONORS: None

FIFA WOMEN'S WORLD CUP™ APPEARANCES: 4

UEFA WOMEN'S CHAMPIONSHIP APPEARANCES: 6

OLYMPIC GAMES APPEARANCES: 2

TOP SCORERS

1.	EUGÉNIE LE SOMMER	86
2.	MARINETTE PICHON	81
3.	MARIE-LAURE DELIE	65
4.	GAËTANE THINEY	58
5.	CAMILLE ABILY	37

LEADING BY EXAMPLE

Current captain Amandine Henry is a linchpin for *Les Bleues*, influencing France's performances from the heart of the midfield. She has played at two FIFA World Cups™ and the UEFA European Championship 2017, winning the adidas Silver Ball at the 2015 FIFA Women's World Cup™.

France women's national soccer team, pictured in 1921.

HISTORY LESSON

The French Football Federation officially recognized women's soccer just fifty years ago, in 1970, although women have played soccer in France since the 1920s. Now, the French men's and women's squads have equal opportunities and share the famous Clairefontaine training facilities.

TOP FINISHER

Prolific forward Eugénie Le Sommer can score with either foot, and she will likely become the nation's all-time leading goalscorer before the UEFA Women's European Championship in 2022. Having made her France debut in 2009, Le Sommer may reach a double century of international caps before she retires.

MOST APPEARANCES

1. SANDRINE SOUBEYRAND	198	
2. ÉLISE BUSSAGLIA	192	
3. LAURA GEORGES	188	
4. CAMILLE ABILY	183	
5. EUGÉNIE LE SOMMER	174	

GERMANY (MEN'S)

Germany are a giant in world soccer with a near-perfect record in FIFA World Cup™ and UEFA European Championship qualification. Among the most successful national sides, they are one of just three teams to have four or more World Cup stars sewn onto their shirts.

In 2014, Germany were crowned world champions for the fourth time.

TEAM FACTS

JOINED FIFA: 1908

HIGHEST FIFA/COCA-COLA WORLD RANKING: 1

STADIUM: Various

HONORS: FIFA World Cup 1954, 1974, 1990, 2014 (winners); UEFA European Championship 1972, 1980, 1996 (winners)

FIFA WORLD CUP™ APPEARANCES: 19

UEFA EUROPEAN CHAMPIONSHIP APPEARANCES: 12

TOP SCORERS

1. MIROSLAV KLOSE	71
2. GERD MÜLLER	68
3. LUKAS PODOLSKI	49
4. RUDI VÖLLER	47
= JÜRGEN KLINSMANN	

UNIFIED TRIUMPH

Germany's fourth world title in 2014 ended a period of eighteen years without a trophy. It was the first time Germany won the FIFA World Cup™ as a unified nation, but they have been crowned world champions in 1954, 1974, and 1990 as West Germany. The 2014 final was a tense affair, with Mario Götze's (below) goal in extra time proving the difference against Argentina.

KLOSE RANGE

Polish-born marksman Miroslav Klose is Germany's all-time top scorer with seventy-one goals. Klose also holds the honor of being the top scorer at the FIFA World Cup™, netting sixteen goals across four tournaments (2002, 2006, 2010, 2014). Remarkably, Germany never lost a game in which Klose scored.

LOTHAR THE LEGEND

Lothar Matthäus (below) had a remarkable international career. He famously captained West Germany to victory at the FIFA World Cup Italy 1990™, and he had been a European Champion ten years earlier with the *Nationalelf* (National Eleven). The combative central midfielder is Germany's most-capped player with 150 international appearances.

MOST APPEARANCES

1. LOTHAR MATTHÄUS	150
2. MIROSLAV KLOSE	137
3. LUKAS PODOLSKI	130
4. BASTIAN SCHWEINSTEIGER	121
5. PHILIPP LAHM	113

GERMANY (WOMEN'S)

The most successful women's national side in Europe, Germany have won the FIFA Women's World Cup™ twice (2003 and 2007) and have clinched the UEFA Women's Championship a record eight times. The team also won Olympic gold at the 2016 Games in Rio de Janeiro.

Along with the USA, Germany have finished in the top eight teams at every FIFA Women's World Cup™.

Germany show off their gold medals following their victory over Sweden at the 2016 Olympic Games.

TEAM FACTS

HIGHEST FIFA/COCA-COLA WOMEN'S WORLD RANKING: 1

HONORS: FIFA Women's World Cup 2003, 2007 (winners); UEFA Women's Championship 1989, 1991, 1995, 1997, 2001, 2005, 2009, 2013 (winners); Olympic Games 2016 (gold medal), 2000, 2004, 2008 (bronze medals)

FIFA WOMEN'S WORLD CUP™ APPEARANCES: 8

UEFA WOMEN'S CHAMPIONSHIP APPEARANCES: 10

OLYMPIC GAMES APPEARANCES: 5

TOP SCORERS

1.	BIRGIT PRINZ	128
2.	HEIDI MOHR	83
3.	INKA GRINGS	64
4.	CÉLIA ŠAŠIĆ	63
5.	ALEXANDRA POPP	53

DOUBLE CROWN

In 2007, Germany entered the FIFA Women's World Cup™ as the reigning champions. Led by Birgit Prinz, the team outclassed their opposition in every game on their route to the final, where they faced Brazil. Legendary goalkeeper Nadine Angerer saved a penalty, as Germany sealed victory without conceding a single goal in the tournament.

SUPER STRIKER

Birgit Prinz (above) is Germany's golden girl. The striker won two FIFA Women's World Cups™, five UEFA Women's Championships, and three Olympic bronze medals with the national side. Prinz made her debut at sixteen in 1994 and went on to make the most international appearances of any female player in Europe. She remains Germany's record goalscorer with 128 strikes to her name.

GERMANY'S RISE

Just like in England, women's soccer in Germany has enjoyed mixed fortunes. In 1955, the German FA banned its teams from allowing women to play the game in West Germany—a ban that lasted until 1970. The national team played their first game in 1982 and finally made their debut (as West Germany) at the 1989 UEFA Women's Championship, which they went on to win.

The Germany squad line up ahead of their semifinal contest against Italy at the UEFA Women's EURO 1989.

MOST APPEARANCES

1. BIRGIT PRINZ	214	
2. KIRSTIN STEGEMANN	191	
3. ARIANE HINGST	174	
4. ANJA MITTAG	158	
5. BETTINA WIEGMANN	154	

ITALY (MEN'S)

Four-time FIFA World Cup™ winners Italy are just one win short of Brazil's record, and have also won the UEFA European Championship twice, in 1968 and 2021 (at EURO 2020). Nicknamed the *Azzurri*, Italy played their first match in 1910, against France.

Italy play in blue ("azzurro" in Italian). The color is associated with the royal dynasty that unified Italy in 1861.

Fabio Cannavaro lifts the trophy after Italy beat France in a penalty shoot-out at the FIFA World Cup Germany 2006™.

TEAM FACTS

JOINED FIFA: 1910

HIGHEST FIFA/COCA-COLA WORLD RANKING: 1

STADIUM: Stadio Olimpico (Rome)

HONORS: FIFA World Cup 1934, 1938, 1982, 2006 (winners); UEFA European Championship 1968, 2021 (EURO 2020) (winners)

FIFA WORLD CUP™ APPEARANCES: 18

UEFA EUROPEAN CHAMPIONSHIP APPEARANCES: 9

TOP SCORERS

1.	LUIGI RIVA	35
2.	GIUSEPPE MEAZZA	33
3.	SILVIO PIOLA	30
4.	ROBERTO BAGGIO	27
=	ALESSANDRO DEL PIERO	

PIONEERING POZZO

Italy coach Vittorio Pozzo (right, holding trophy) is the only head coach in the men's game to have won the FIFA World Cup™ twice, in 1934 and 1938. These wins sandwiched an Olympic gold medal win at the 1936 Games in Berlin. Pozzo is regarded as a pioneer of world soccer and was regarded as a master tactician.

4 - CAMPIONATI MONDIALI DI CALCIO

NOVO: il brodo ricco di 12 saporiti ingredienti

Riproduzione vietata   Spiegazione a tergo

LEADING FROM THE BACK

Legendary Italian captain Gianluigi Buffon (left) is considered to be among the most gifted goalkeepers to have ever played the game. He holds the record for the most appearances for Italy with 176 caps, and featured in the national squad at five FIFA World Cups™ (a winner in 2006), four UEFA European Championships, and the 1996 Olympic Games.

CENTURION CAPTAIN

Centerback Fabio Cannavaro (below) led Italy to victory at the 2006 FIFA World Cup Germany™—the last time they won the trophy. He was named FIFA World Player of the Year in the same year, becoming the first defender to win the award. Cannavaro featured for the *Azzurri* 136 times, which is a record number of caps for an outfield player.

MOST APPEARANCES

1. GIANLUIGI BUFFON	176
2. FABIO CANNAVARO	136
3. PAOLO MALDINI	126
4. DANIELE DE ROSSI	117
5. ANDREA PIRLO	116

69

NETHERLANDS (MEN'S)

The *Oranje* (the Orange) are known for their entertaining brand of "Total Soccer," where every player must have strong technical skills. Their only major trophy was won at the UEFA European Championship in 1988, but they have been FIFA World Cup™ runners-up three times.

The Netherlands team that finished as runners-up in the UEFA Nations League final in 2019.

TEAM FACTS

JOINED FIFA: 1905

HIGHEST FIFA/COCA-COLA WORLD RANKING: 1

STADIUM: Johan Cruyff Arena (Amsterdam)

HONORS: FIFA World Cup 1974, 1978, 2010 (runners-up); UEFA European Championship 1988 (winner)

FIFA WORLD CUP™ APPEARANCES: 10

UEFA EUROPEAN CHAMPIONSHIP APPEARANCES: 9

TOP SCORERS

1. ROBIN VAN PERSIE	50
2. KLAAS-JAN HUNTELAAR	42
3. PATRICK KLUIVERT	40
4. DENNIS BERGKAMP	37
= ARJEN ROBBEN	

DUTCH MASTER

Johan Cruyff (below) is a soccer icon. His style of play and soccer philosophy have inspired many players and managers in world soccer. The skillful attacker played for his country forty-eight times and scored thirty-three goals. His famous trick, the "Cruyff turn," confused defenders and wowed crowds and television audiences worldwide.

FINAL FRUSTRATION

The Netherlands came closest to becoming world champions in 2010. They were in sparkling form as they won every game to reach the final, where they faced Spain. All square after 90 minutes, Spain's Andreas Iniesta struck in the second period of extra time to break Dutch hearts.

ROBIN'S RECORD

Left-footed forward Robin van Persie (below, right) is the Netherlands' record goalscorer, with fifty goals from 102 international appearances. The Flying Dutchman represented his country at the FIFA World Cup™ in 2006, 2010, and 2014, and at the UEFA European Championship in 2008 and 2012.

MOST APPEARANCES

1. WESLEY SNEIJDER	134
2. EDWIN VAN DER SAR	130
3. FRANK DE BOER	112
4. RAFAEL VAN DER VAART	109
5. GIOVANNI VAN BRONCKHORST	106

NETHERLANDS (WOMEN'S)

The popularity of women's soccer exploded in the Netherlands following the Orange Lionesses' unexpected victory at the UEFA Women's EURO 2017. The Dutch side built on this success by reaching the final of the FIFA Women's World Cup 2019™ in France two years later.

Women's soccer is the fastest growing sport in the Netherlands, with a total membership of 1.2 million players.

The Netherlands squad ahead of the final of the FIFA Women's World Cup 2019™.

TEAM FACTS

HIGHEST FIFA/COCA-COLA WOMEN'S WORLD RANKING: 2

HONORS: UEFA Women's Championship 2017 (winners); FIFA Women's World Cup 2019 (runners-up)

FIFA WOMEN'S WORLD CUP™ APPEARANCES: 2

UEFA WOMEN'S CHAMPIONSHIP APPEARANCES: 3

OLYMPIC GAMES APPEARANCES: –

TOP SCORERS

1. VIVIANNE MIEDEMA	73
2. MANON MELIS	59
3. LIEKE MARTENS	49
4. SHERIDA SPITSE	42
5. SYLVIA SMIT	30

LOYAL FOLLOWING

Legions of Dutch fans have supported the Orange Lionesses' rapid rise to the top in recent years. Thousands celebrated following the Netherlands' shock win at the UEFA Women's EURO 2017. The team's final against the USA in 2019 was the most-watched game in the FIFA Women's World Cup™ history, with a worldwide television audience of more than 82 million viewers.

LONG-TIME LEADER

Nearing a double century of international caps, defensive midfielder Sherida Spitse has been a regular name in the Dutch side since making her debut against England in 2006. She forms the anchor in the Dutch midfield and captained the side to their European title in 2017.

EURO STAR

Striker Vivianne Miedema, who made her international debut at seventeen, is already the team's record goalscorer. She was a key player in the Dutch side's victory at UEFA Women's EURO 2017 and got her name into the history books by scoring in the semifinal and twice in the final against Denmark.

MOST APPEARANCES

1. SHERIDA SPITSE	188
2. ANNEMIEKE KIESEL	156
3. DYANNE BITO	146
4. MARLEEN WISSINK	141
5. DAPHNE KOSTER	139

SPAIN (MEN'S)

Spain were crowned world champions for the first time in 2010, adding to the UEFA European Championship they won two years earlier. A second European crown was secured in 2012 as Spain reigned supreme during a golden age in their history.

Luis Suárez Miramontes is the oldest player to represent the nation at almost 37 years old (36 years, 346 days).

Spain celebrate becoming world champions at the FIFA World Cup 2010™.

TEAM FACTS

JOINED FIFA: 1920	
HIGHEST FIFA/COCA-COLA WORLD RANKING: 1	
STADIUM: various	
HONORS: FIFA World Cup 2010 (winners); UEFA European Championship 1964, 2008, 2012 (winners); Olympic Games 1920 (silver medal)	
FIFA WORLD CUP™ APPEARANCES: 15	
UEFA EUROPEAN CHAMPIONSHIP APPEARANCES: 10	

TOP SCORERS

1.	DAVID VILLA	59
2.	RAÚL	44
3.	FERNANDO TORRES	38
4.	DAVID SILVA	35
5.	FERNANDO HIERRO	29

LONG-SERVING DEFENDER

Spain's No. 15, Sergio Ramos (below), has been a loyal servant to his country, reaching a record number of caps and scoring more than twenty goals—a fantastic return for a centerback. Ramos was world champion with Spain in 2010 and a double European champion in 2008 and 2012. He took over the Spain captaincy in 2016 and led the side until 2021.

GOAL KING

David Villa is Spain's leading marksman, scoring fifty-nine goals. The striker won the adidas Golden Boot as Spain triumphed at UEFA EURO 2008 and earned the adidas Silver Boot at the FIFA World Cup South Africa 2010™ as joint top scorer (with fewer assists than the winner Thomas Müller). Sadly, a broken leg forced Villa out of the squad that won EURO 2012.

GOLDEN GENERATION

The group of players that won the FIFA World Cup™ and two European titles over five magical years (2008-2012) is classed among the greatest squads of all time. With Iker Casillas in goal, the rock-solid duo of Sergio Ramos and Raúl Albiol in defense, the fantastic Iniesta and Xavi in midfield, and David Villa and Fernando Torres (right) up front, the team were almost impossible to beat.

MOST APPEARANCES

1. SERGIO RAMOS	180	
2. IKER CASILLAS	167	
3. XAVI	133	
4. ANDRÉS INIESTA	131	
5. SERGIO BUSQUETS	127	

BELGIUM (MEN'S)

Belgium's current squad is full of talent, which helped them reach the top of the FIFA World Rankings in 2015 and regain it in 2018. Players such as Eden Hazard, Kevin de Bruyne, and Romelu Lukaku have been key to their success.

TEAM FACTS

JOINED FIFA: 1904

HIGHEST FIFA/COCA COLA WORLD RANKING: 1

STADIUM: Various

HONORS: UEFA European Championship 1980 (runners-up); FIFA World Cup 2018 (third place)

FIFA WORLD CUP™ APPEARANCES: 13

UEFA EUROPEAN CHAMPIONSHIP APPEARANCES: 5

MOST APPEARANCES

JAN VERTONGHEN — 131

TOP SCORER

ROMELU LUKAKU — 64

CROATIA (MEN'S)

Croatia were FIFA members briefly during the 1940s, but played most of last century as Yugoslavia. They rejoined FIFA in 1992 and have excelled since. Most recently they reached the final of the 2018 FIFA World Cup™.

TEAM FACTS

JOINED FIFA: 1992

HIGHEST FIFA/COCA-COLA WORLD RANKING: 3

STADIUM: Various

HONORS: FIFA World Cup 2018 (runners-up)

FIFA WORLD CUP™ APPEARANCES: 5

UEFA EUROPEAN CHAMPIONSHIP APPEARANCES: 5

MOST APPEARANCES

LUKA MODRIĆ — 142

TOP SCORER

DAVOR ŠUKER — 45

GREECE (MEN'S)

Greece surprised everyone when they became the ninth nation to be crowned European champions in 2004. The tournament was only Greece's second appearance in the competition, as they stunned hosts Portugal with a 1–0 victory in the final.

TEAM FACTS

JOINED FIFA: 1929	
HIGHEST FIFA/COCA-COLA WORLD RANKING: 7	
STADIUM: Olympic Stadium (Athens)	
HONORS: UEFA European Championship 2004 (winners)	
FIFA WORLD CUP™ APPEARANCES: 3	
UEFA EUROPEAN CHAMPIONSHIP APPEARANCES: 4	

MOST APPEARANCES

GIORGOS KARAGOUNIS	139

TOP SCORER

NIKOS ANASTOPOULOS	29

PORTUGAL (MEN'S)

Portugal joined FIFA almost a century ago, but had to wait until 2016 to claim their first major European trophy. A UEFA Nations League title followed soon after in 2019, with record-breaking scorer Cristiano Ronaldo at the heart of Portugal's success.

TEAM FACTS

JOINED FIFA: 1921	
HIGHEST FIFA/COCA-COLA WORLD RANKING: 3	
STADIUM: Estádio da Luz (Lisbon)	
HONORS: UEFA European Championship 2016 (winners); UEFA Nations League 2019 (winners)	
FIFA WORLD CUP™ APPEARANCES: 7	
UEFA EUROPEAN CHAMPIONSHIP APPEARANCES: 7	

MOST APPEARANCES

CRISTIANO RONALDO	179

TOP SCORER

CRISTIANO RONALDO	109

NORWAY (WOMEN'S)

Norway spearheaded the global spread of women's soccer, with triumphs in Europe and on the world stage. Midfielder and record caps holder Hege Riise was one of Norway's brightest stars, helping her country to win three major international honors between 1995 and 2000.

Norway were European Championship finalists four times in a row between 1987 and 1993.

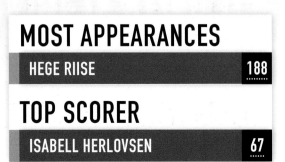

Norway celebrate beating the USA to win Olympic gold at the 2000 Games in Sydney.

TEAM FACTS

HIGHEST FIFA/COCA-COLA WOMEN'S WORLD RANKING: 2

HONORS: FIFA Women's World Cup 1995 (winners); UEFA Women's Championship 1987, 1993 (winners); Olympic Games 2000 (gold medal), 1996 (bronze medal)

FIFA WOMEN'S WORLD CUP™ APPEARANCES: 8

UEFA WOMEN'S CHAMPIONSHIP APPEARANCES: 11

OLYMPIC GAMES APPEARANCES: 3

MOST APPEARANCES

HEGE RIISE	188

TOP SCORER

ISABELL HERLOVSEN	67

SWEDEN (WOMEN'S)

The *Blue and Yellows* have played in every FIFA Women's World Cup™, and narrowly missed out on major honors in the 2003 final, when Germany scored a golden goal in extra time. Sweden won the UEFA Women's Championship in 1984.

Sweden beat England to finish third at 2019 FIFA Women's World Cup ™.

TEAM FACTS

HIGHEST FIFA/COCA-COLA WOMEN'S WORLD RANKING: 3
HONORS: FIFA Women's World Cup 2003 (runners-up); UEFA Women's Championship 1984 (winners); Olympic Games 2016 (silver medal)
FIFA WOMEN'S WORLD CUP™ APPEARANCES: 8
UEFA WOMEN'S CHAMPIONSHIP APPEARANCES: 10
OLYMPIC GAMES APPEARANCES: 6

MOST APPEARANCES

THERESE SJÖGRAN	214

TOP SCORER

LOTTA SCHELIN	88

MEXICO (MEN'S)

Mexico have qualified for the FIFA World Cup™ sixteen times, reaching the quarterfinals in 1970 and 1986. Fierce rivals of the USA, Mexico have won the Concacaf Gold Cup eleven times. Often unpredictable, their biggest margin of defeat was 8–0 against England in 1961.

The Mexico lineup ahead of their 2018 FIFA World Cup Russia™ group stage game against Germany.

TEAM FACTS

JOINED FIFA: 1929

HIGHEST FIFA/COCA-COLA WORLD RANKING: 4

STADIUM: Various

HONORS: Concacaf Championship/Gold Cup (11 wins)

FIFA WORLD CUP™ APPEARANCES: 16

MOST APPEARANCES
CLAUDIO SUÁREZ 177

TOP SCORER
JAVIER HERNÁNDEZ 52

 # USA (MEN'S)

The USA played their first official international against Sweden in 1916. In 1930, they appeared at the first-ever FIFA World Cup™ and finished in third place—a result they have not equaled since. The USA have won their regional championship, the Concacaf Gold Cup, six times.

The USA reached the quarterfinals of the 2002 FIFA World Cup Korea/Japan™.

The USA hosted the fifteenth edition of the FIFA World Cup™ in 1994, losing to champions Brazil 1–0 in the round of 16.

TEAM FACTS

JOINED FIFA: 1914

HIGHEST FIFA/COCA-COLA WORLD RANKING: 4

STADIUM: Various

HONORS: FIFA World Cup 1930 (third place); Olympic Games 1904 (silver & bronze medals — not sanctioned by FIFA); Concacaf Championship/Gold Cup (6 wins)

FIFA WORLD CUP™ APPEARANCES: 10

MOST APPEARANCES

COBI JONES	164

TOP SCORERS

CLINT DEMPSEY, LANDON DONOVAN	57

USA (WOMEN'S)

The USA are the most successful international women's team, having won the FIFA Women's World Cup™ four times and four Olympic gold medals. Formed in 1985, the USA have helped raise the profile of women's soccer on the global stage over the last few decades.

USA celebrate their opening goal against the Netherlands in the final of the FIFA Women's World Cup 2019™.

The USA and Canada are the leading women's sides in the Concacaf region. Both teams regularly feature in the top ten FIFA/Coca-Cola Women's World rankings.

TEAM FACTS

HIGHEST FIFA/COCA-COLA WOMEN'S WORLD RANKING: 1	
HONORS: FIFA World Cup 1991, 1999, 2015, 2019 (winners), 2011 (runners-up); Olympic Games 1996, 2004, 2008, 2012 (gold medal), 2000 (silver medal)	
FIFA WOMEN'S WORLD CUP™ APPEARANCES: 8	
OLYMPIC GAMES APPEARANCES: 6	

MOST APPEARANCES

KRISTINE LILLY	354

TOP SCORER

ABBY WAMBACH	184

CANADA (WOMEN'S)

Founded in 1986, the Canadian team have played in every World Cup since 1995, and have won two Olympic bronze medals, at the 2012 and 2016 Games. Their national treasure is Christine Sinclair, who is Canada's most capped player as well as all-time leading goalscorer.

Canada reached the round of 16 at theFIFA Women's World Cup France 2019™.

TEAM FACTS

HIGHEST FIFA/COCA-COLA WOMEN'S WORLD RANKING: 4

HONORS: Olympic Games 2012, 2016 (bronze medal)

FIFA WOMEN'S WORLD CUP™ APPEARANCES: 7

OLYMPIC GAMES APPEARANCES: 3

MOST APPEARANCES

CHRISTINE SINCLAIR	299

TOP SCORER

CHRISTINE SINCLAIR	186

ARGENTINA (MEN'S)

Among the oldest national teams in the world, Argentina played their first international game in 1901. The *Albiceleste* (White and Sky Blues) have won the FIFA World Cup™ twice and have finished as runners-up three times—most recently in 2014.

Lionel Messi is the only men's player to have scored at the FIFA World Cup™ in his teens, twenties, and thirties (at the 2006, 2014, and 2018 contests).

Diego Maradona lifts the FIFA World Cup™ trophy following Argentina's famous victory at the 1986 contest.

TEAM FACTS

JOINED FIFA: 1912

HIGHEST FIFA/COCA–COLA WORLD RANKING: 1

STADIUM: Estadio Monumental Antonio Vespucci Liberti (Buenos Aires)

HONORS: FIFA World Cup 1978, 1986 (winners); Copa América (winners — 15 times); FIFA Confederations Cup 1992

FIFA WORLD CUP™ APPEARANCES: 17

CONMEBOL COPA AMÉRICA APPEARANCES: 42

TOP SCORERS

1. LIONEL MESSI	76
2. GABRIEL BATISTUTA	54
3. SERGIO AGÜERO	41
4. HERNÁN CRESPO	35
5. DIEGO MARADONA	34

MESSI UNMATCHED

Six-time winner of the FIFA Ballon d'Or, Lionel Messi is one of the greatest players of all time, At international level, Messi reached seventy goals in 138 appearances in 2019, and has captained the side since 2011. Messi announced his international retirement in 2016 at the age of just twenty-nine, but later changed his mind.

OLYMPIC SUCCESS

Argentina won back-to-back Olympic Gold medals—in Athens 2004 and Beijing 2008. The talented 2008 squad included young players such as Lionel Messi, Sergio Agüero, and Javier Mascherano, all of whom went on to feature among the nation's most celebrated players of all time.

HAND OF GOD

While many consider the late Diego Maradona a national legend, the attacking midfielder had a colorful international career. Not selected for Argentina's FIFA World Cup™-winning side in 1978, Maradona was sent off at the 1982 games. He steered his country to a second crown in 1986, scoring the controversial "Hand of God"goal with his arm.

MOST APPEARANCES

1. LIONEL MESSI	151
2. JAVIER MASCHERANO	147
3. JAVIER ZANETTI	143
4. ROBERTO AYALA	114
5. ÁNGEL DI MARÍA	111

BRAZIL (MEN'S)

Known for their silky skills and creative play, Brazil are always counted among the favorites in any competition. They have claimed the FIFA World Cup™ Trophy a record five times. The team also won gold at the 2016 Olympic Games, which were held on home turf in Rio.

Brazil captain Cafu lifts the FIFA World Cup Trophy in 2002 after their record fifth win.

TEAM FACTS

JOINED FIFA: 1923

HIGHEST FIFA/COCA-COLA WORLD RANKING: 1

STADIUM: Maracanã (Rio de Janeiro)

HONORS: FIFA World Cup 1958, 1962, 1970, 1994, 2002 (winners); Copa América (winners—9 times); FIFA Confederations Cup 1997, 2005, 2009, 2013 (winners); Olympic Games 2016 (gold medal), 1984, 1988, 2012 (silver medals).

FIFA WORLD CUP™ APPEARANCES: 21

CONMEBOL COPA AMÉRICA APPEARANCES: 37

TOP SCORERS

1. PELÉ	77
2. NEYMAR JR	68
3. RONALDO	62
4. ROMÁRIO	55
5. ZICO	48

MOST APPEARANCES

1.	CAFU	142
2.	ROBERTO CARLOS	125
3.	DANI ALVES	118
4.	LÚCIO	105
5.	NEYMAR JR	101

SWAPPING SHIRTS

Brazil's bright yellow shirts are famous throughout the world. The top has even earned the team the nickname—the *Canarinha* (Little Canary). Prior to the FIFA World Cup™ in 1954, the team wore white shirts tipped with blue. Brazil first became world champions in 1958 wearing blue, so as not to clash with finalists Sweden's colors.

KING PELÉ

Brazil legend Pelé (below) can boast the title of joint FIFA Player of the Century (alongside Argentina's Diego Maradona). Pelé played in four World Cups and remains the only player to have won the trophy three times. He first became world champion at the 1958 FIFA World Cup Sweden™, at seventeen. Pelé is still the nation's all-time top scorer, even though he won his final cap in 1971, almost fifty years ago.

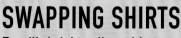

CAPTAIN FANTASTIC

Cafu (below) holds the men's record for the most games played for Brazil. The fast fullback is remembered for his roving runs and expertly timed tackles. He played in three FIFA World Cup™ tournaments, lifting the trophy as captain in 2002. The last of his 142 caps came at the FIFA World Cup Germany 2006™, as Brazil bowed out at the quarterfinal stage.

Brazilian players are known by their first names or nicknames —a tradition that dates to 1914. Pelé's full name is Edson Arantes do Nascimento.

BRAZIL (WOMEN'S)

The national women's team of Brazil played their first game in 1986 and have featured at every FIFA Women's World Cup™ since the tournament began in 1991. The *Canarinhas* have come close to glory three times, finishing as finalists at the tournament in 2007 and winning Olympic silver at both the 2004 and 2008 Games.

Brazil are pictured before capturing the silver medal at the 2008 Olympic Games.

TEAM FACTS

HIGHEST FIFA/COCA-COLA WOMEN'S WORLD RANKING: 2

HONORS: FIFA Women's World Cup 2007 (runners-up); Olympic Games 2004, 2008 (silver medals)

FIFA WOMEN'S WORLD CUP™ APPEARANCES: 8

OLYMPIC GAMES APPEARANCES: 6

TOP SCORERS

1.	MARTA	109
2.	CRISTIANE	96
3.	ROSELI	42
=	PRETINHA	
5.	DEBINHA	40

MARVELOUS MARTA

Marta Vieira da Silva (below) is Brazil's most iconic player and one of the greatest female players of all time. Her record goals tally for Brazil and appearances at five FIFA Women's World Cups and four Olympic Games have earned her The FIFA Best Women's Player award multiple times over a long and stellar career.

FAMOUS FORMIGA

Midfielder Formiga (left) is a record breaker. She has played at the FIFA Women's World Cup™ a record seven times over twenty-four years and has taken part in all six contests of the Women's Olympic Soccer tournament. At forty-one years and 112 days, she became the oldest player to have appeared at a FIFA Women's World Cup™ and is the competition's oldest goalscorer, too.

Brazil are the most successful women's nation in South America, having won seven out of eight contests of the *Copa América Femenina*.

BRAZILIAN BAN

The history of women's soccer in Brazil is similar to that of many European nations. In 1941, Brazil's president banned women from playing soccer, deciding the sport was "incompatible with the conditions of the feminine nature." The ban remained in place until 1979, when progress in the women's game could finally be made.

MOST APPEARANCES

1.	FORMIGA	200
2.	MARTA	157
3.	CRISTIANE	150
4.	ROSANA	114
5.	TAMIRES	108

URUGUAY (MEN'S)

Uruguay won the very first FIFA World Cup™ in 1930. They won it a second time twenty years later, at the 1950 contest, and are the smallest nation to have lifted the trophy. A joint record fifteen *Copa América* titles complete this nation's proud soccer pedigree.

Uruguay's Edinson Cavani (21) celebrates scoring against Russia at the 2018 FIFA World Cup Russia™.

Uruguay's historic home stadium, Estadio Centenario, was built for the first FIFA World Cup™ in 1930. At one time its capacity was almost 100,000.

TEAM FACTS

JOINED FIFA: 1916

HIGHEST FIFA/COCA-COLA WORLD RANKING: 2

STADIUM: Estadio Centenario (Montevideo)

HONORS: FIFA World Cup 1930, 1950 (winners); Olympic Games 1924, 1928 (gold medal); Copa América (winners—15 times)

FIFA WORLD CUP™ APPEARANCES: 13

COPA AMÉRICA APPEARANCES: 44

TOP SCORERS

1. LUIS SUÁREZ	64
2. EDINSON CAVANI	53
3. DIEGO FORLÁN	36
4. HÉCTOR SCARONE	31
5. ÁNGEL ROMANO	28

COPA CHAMPIONS

With a population of fewer than 3.5 million, Uruguay are the third-smallest nation in South America. Despite their size, Uruguay have won their continental championship, the CONMEBOL *Copa América*, more times than anyone else. *La Celeste* (The Sky Blue) lead the way with fifteen titles, while neighbors Argentina have fourteen.

OLYMPIC DOUBLE

Uruguay have twice featured at the Olympic Games: in 1924 (Paris) and 1928 (Amsterdam), winning the gold medal at both tournaments. Héctor Scarone (circled below) was key to Uruguay's success, striking five times in Paris and three in Amsterdam. The forward remains the nation's fourth top scorer, with thirty-one goals in fifty-two games.

GOLDEN GODÍN

Ranked among the best defenders in the world, no player has featured more times for Uruguay than captain Diego Godín (below). He made his international debut at nineteen, and has since appeared at the FIFA World Cup™ three times. Godín was made captain in 2015 and has played more than 130 times for his country.

MOST APPEARANCES

1. DIEGO GODÍN	146
2. MAXI PEREIRA	125
3. EDINSON CAVANI	123
= FERNANDO MUSLERA	123
= LUIS SUÁREZ	123

LEADING AFRICAN NATIONS (MEN'S)

A total of thirteen different African nations have featured at a men's FIFA World Cup™, with three teams from sub-Saharan Africa having reached the quarterfinal stage—Cameroon, Senegal, and Ghana. CAF's regional trophy is the Africa Cup of Nations (AFCON).

Cameroon were the first African team to reach the FIFA World Cup™ quarterfinals, in 1990.

Egypt was the first nation from Africa to make an appearance at the FIFA World Cup™, in the 1934 contest hosted in Italy.

AFRICAN REGIONAL FEDERATIONS

- UNAF (NORTH AFRICA)
- WAFU-UFOA (WEST AFRICA)
- UNIFFAC (CENTRAL AFRICA)
- CECAFA (EAST AFRICA)
- COSAFA (SOUTHERN AFRICA)

TOP SCORERS

1. GODFREY CHITALU (ZAMBIA)	79
2. KINNAH PHIRI (MALAWI)	71
3. HOSSAM HASSAN (EGYPT)	69
4. DIDIER DROGBA (IVORY COAST)	65
5 SAMUEL ETO'O (CAMEROON)	56

MOST APPEARANCES

1. AHMED HASSAN (EGYPT)	184
2. HOSSAM HASSAN (EGYPT)	170
3. ESSAM EL HADARY (EGYPT)	159
= YOUNG CHIMODZI (MALAWI)	159
4. RIGOBERT SONG (CAMEROON)	137

Cameroon's Roger Milla is the oldest goalscorer in FIFA World Cup™ history. He was forty-two years, 39 days when he netted against Russia in 1994.

OLYMPIC GLORY

African nations Cameroon, Ghana, and Nigeria have all tasted Olympic success, winning between them a total of five Olympic soccer medals in the men's soccer tournament. Nigeria exceled on the world stage, claiming gold in 1996, with Cameroon beating Argentina to top the podium four years later at the Games in Sydney.

Nigeria celebrate winning gold in the Olympic men's soccer event at the 1996 Games in Atlanta.

JAPAN (MEN'S)

The *Samurai Blue* jointly hosted the FIFA World Cup™ in 2002 with Korea Republic, and reached the second round for the first time in their history that year. Among the region's strongest sides, they have won the AFC Asian Cup four times.

TEAM FACTS

JOINED FIFA: 1950	
HIGHEST FIFA/COCA-COLA WORLD RANKING: 9	
STADIUM: Various	
HONORS: AFC Asian Cup 1992, 2000, 2004, 2011 (winners); Olympic Games 1968 (bronze medal)	
FIFA WORLD CUP™ APPEARANCES: 6	

MOST APPEARANCES

YASUHITO ENDŌ	152

TOP SCORER

KUNISHIGE KAMAMOTO	75

KOREA REPUBLIC (MEN'S)

Korea Republic have featured in ten FIFA World Cup™ final rounds, playing an Asian record thirty-four games. Their best performance in the contest came when they co-hosted the tournament in 2002. The *Reds'* impressive run saw them become the first Asian side to reach the semifinals.

TEAM FACTS

JOINED FIFA: 1948	
HIGHEST FIFA/COCA-COLA WORLD RANKING: 17	
STADIUM: Seoul World Cup Stadium (Seoul)	
HONORS: AFC Asian Cup 1956, 1960 (winners)	
FIFA WORLD CUP™ APPEARANCES: 10	

MOST APPEARANCES

CHA BUM-KUN (A), HONG MYUNG-BO	136

TOP SCORER

CHA BUM-KUN	58

JAPAN (WOMEN'S)

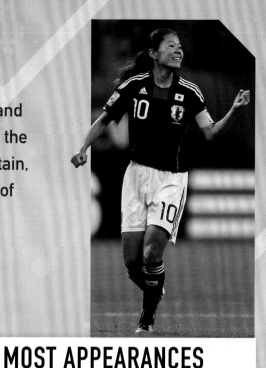

Japan are the most successful women's national side in Asia and have appeared at every FIFA Women's World Cup™. They won the trophy in a shock victory over the USA in 2011, led by their captain, Homare Sawa (right). The former FIFA Women's World Player of the Year tops Japan's tables for both appearances and goals.

TEAM FACTS

HIGHEST FIFA/COCA-COLA WOMEN'S WORLD RANKING: 3

HONORS: FIFA Women's World Cup 2011 (winners); AFC Women's Asian Cup 2014, 2018 (winners); Olympic Games 2012 (silver medal)

FIFA WOMEN'S WORLD CUP™ APPEARANCES: 8

OLYMPIC GAMES APPEARANCES: 4

MOST APPEARANCES

HOMARE SAWA	205

TOP SCORER

HOMARE SAWA	83

CHINA PR (WOMEN'S)

China were a pioneering nation as the women's game began to go global in the 1990s. They hosted the first FIFA Women's World Cup™ in 1991 and claimed the runners-up spot in 1999, narrowly losing to the USA in a penalty shoot-out. Sun Wen was one of the team's brightest stars during China's golden age.

TEAM FACTS

HIGHEST FIFA/COCA-COLA WOMEN'S WORLD RANKING: 4

HONORS: FIFA Women's World Cup 1999 (runners-up); Olympic Games 1996 (silver medal); AFC Women's Asian Cup (winners—8 times)

FIFA WOMEN'S WORLD CUP™ APPEARANCES: 7

OLYMPIC GAMES APPEARANCES: 4

MOST APPEARANCES

PUI WEI	219

TOP SCORER

SUN WEN	106

AUSTRALIA (MEN'S)

Australia belonged to OFC until 2006, when they switched to the Asian Football Confederation. The Socceroos have qualified for the last four FIFA World Cup™ competitions and reached the round of 16 in 2006—their best position. Their biggest rivals in the AFC region are Japan.

Australia have begun their qualifying campaign for the 2022 FIFA World Cup Qatar™.

TEAM FACTS

JOINED FIFA: 1963

HIGHEST FIFA/COCA-COLA WORLD RANKING: 14

STADIUM: Various

HONORS: AFC Asian Cup 2015 (winners); OFC Nations Cup 1980, 1996, 2000, 2004 (winners)

FIFA WORLD CUP™ APPEARANCES: 5

MOST APPEARANCES

MARK SCHWARZER	109

TOP SCORER

TIM CAHILL	50

AUSTRALIA (WOMEN'S)

Founded in 1978, the women's national team made modest progress, failing to qualify for the first FIFA Women's World Cup™ in 1991. Since then, the Matildas have qualified for the tournament every time, reaching the quarterfinals on three occasions. Australia now belong to the AFC, where they won their first regional championship in 2010.

TEAM FACTS

HIGHEST FIFA/COCA-COLA WOMEN'S WORLD RANKING: 4

HONORS: OFC Women's Championship 1994, 1998, 2003 (winners); AFC Women's Asian Cup 2010 (winners)

FIFA WOMEN'S WORLD CUP™ APPEARANCES: 7

OLYMPIC GAMES APPEARANCES: 2

MOST APPEARANCES

CHERYL SALISBURY | 151

TOP SCORER

LISA DE VANNA | 47

OFC TEAMS

Eleven nations are currently full members of OFC, from American Samoa to Vanatu. Following Australia's departure to join the AFC in 2006, New Zealand became the most successful nation in the OFC. The All Whites have qualified for the FIFA World Cup™ twice and won the OFC Cup five times.

New Zealand have played in both the women's and men's contests of the FIFA World Cup™.

FIFA Women's World Cup™ saw New Zealand make their fifth appearance at the competition in 2019.

CONTINENTAL TOURNAMENTS

Each season the domestic leagues and cup winners earn the right to compete in even greater sports challenges. Annual tournaments such as the UEFA Champions League decide Europe's best teams each year, while the CONMEBOL *Copa Libertadores* competition determines the team champions in South America.

Fans show their support as the teams line up ahead of the UEFA Champions League round of 16 second-leg game between FC Barcelona and Paris Saint-Germain at Camp Nou in 2017.

UEFA CHAMPIONS LEAGUE

Team competitions do not come any bigger than the UEFA Champions League. The top teams from Europe's strongest leagues have taken part in the competition every year since it was first staged in 1955.

The 2015 final was the most-watched game in UEFA Champions League history. The game between Juventus and FC Barcelona drew an average global TV viewing figure of 180 million.

Spanish team Real Madrid celebrate their UEFA Champions League victory in 2018.

MOST WINS

👕	REAL MADRID	13

MOST APPEARANCES

👕	REAL MADRID	51

TOURNAMENT FACTS

HISTORY	YEAR	TEAMS
FIRST EDITION	1955/56	16
LATEST EDITION	2020/21	32
NEXT EDITION	2021/22	32

TOURNAMENT FORMAT

The first round of the UEFA Champions League is a group stage featuring thirty-two teams split into eight groups of four. The winners and runners-up of each group advance to the knockout phases. The knockout games are played until two teams remain to contest the dramatic final at a venue that is chosen in advance of the tournament.

SCORING SENSATION

With 135 strikes, Cristiano Ronaldo is the leading scorer in the competition's history. He earned his record playing for three different teams in three different countries: Manchester United (England), Real Madrid (Spain), and Juventus (Italy).

FANTASTIC FINALS

Over the years, the UEFA Champions League has produced some unforgettable finals, which have seen some of the greatest teams battle spectacularly to win the famous UEFA Champions League Trophy. Here are some of the most memorable finals in the history of the tournament.

Milan Might (1994) ▼

AC Milan 4–0 FC Barcelona

Staged in Athens, the 1994 final saw underdogs AC Milan produce a superb performance to demolish giants FC Barcelona. The *Rossoneri* were two goals up at halftime, They struck twice more in the second half to cruise to victory and claim their fifth European crown.

Red Devils rally (1999) ▲

Manchester United 2–1 Bayern Munich

The atmosphere was electric at the Camp Nou in 1999, as Bayern Munich looked to have all but sealed victory with an early goal. With three minutes of injury time left to play, Manchester United pushed for an equalizer. Teddy Sheringham tapped in goal number one before substitute Ole Gunnar Solskjær struck again to complete a comeback that left Bayern heartbroken.

The Night in Istanbul (2005) ▼

AC Milan 3–3 Liverpool
(Liverpool won 3-2 on penalties)

In the 2005 final, Liverpool completed a stunning comeback. The Reds were 3–0 down at halftime to Italian side AC Milan, but fought back with goals from Steven Gerrard, Vladimir Šmicer, and Xabi Alonso, scored six minutes apart, to take the game into extra time and penalties. Liverpool won the shoot-out to earn the team's fifth trophy. The Reds would triumph again in 2019.

THE UEFA CHAMPIONS LEAGUE TROPHY

The current trophy is the fifth version of the classic design. The cup is 29 inches tall and weighs 16.5 pounds. Previously, a rule stated that the cup became the property of any team who won the competition either five times or three years in a row. Real Madrid, AC Milan, Ajax, and Liverpool all have a version in their trophy cabinets. UEFA changed the rule in 2008 and now awards teams a replica trophy.

Only twenty-two teams have won the Champions League since the tournament began in 1955.

UEFA WOMEN'S CHAMPIONS LEAGUE

The top team competition for women in Europe is the UEFA Women's Champions League. The tournament was first played in 2001 under the name the "UEFA Women's Cup," It was renamed for the 2009/10 contest.

Lyon's Ada Hegerberg (below) became the competition's leading scorer in 2019 with 53 goals.

In 2019, Lyon became the first team to play 100 UEFA Women's Cup/ Champions League games, adding to their record six titles.

French side Lyon have been crowned European champions six times—more than any other team.

MOST WINS	
LYON	7
MOST APPEARANCES	
KÍ KLAKSVÍK	15

TOURNAMENT FACTS

HISTORY	YEAR	TEAMS
FIRST EDITION	2001/02	32
LATEST EDITION	2020/21	32
NEXT EDITION	2021/22	73

ALL-TIME TOURNAMENT WINNERS

TEAM		YEARS
👕	LYON	2011, 2012, 2016, 2017, 2018, 2019, 2020
👕	FFC FRANKFURT	2002, 2006, 2008, 2015
👕	UMEÅ	2003, 2004
👕	TURBINE POTSDAM	2005, 2010
👕	WOLFSBURG	2013, 2014

FIRST FOR FRANKFURT

German side Frankfurt, led by Birgit Prinz (below center), were the first UEFA Women's Cup winners in 2002. Played in Frankfurt's home city, the final was attended by more than 12,000 fans, setting a new European attendance record for a women's team fixture at the time.

TRIPLE TRIUMPH

Retired forward Conny Pohlers (left) has been a European champion with three German clubs: Turbine Potsdam (2005), FFC Frankfurt (2008), and Wolfsburg (2013 and 2014).

QUICK OFF THE MARK

Brazilian Marta scored for Umeå after just twelve seconds in the first leg of the 2008 final at home. Sadly for Umeå, Frankfurt edged the contest, winning 4–3 in total goals.

UEFA EUROPA LEAGUE

Held annually, the UEFA Europa League offers teams the chance to win a major European trophy. The competition was first staged in 1971 when it was known as the UEFA Cup. Teams qualify for the competition based on their final positions across the top leagues in Europe.

Villarreal claimed their first Europa League title in 2021, beating Manchester United 11–10 in an exciting penalty shoot-out.

TOURNAMENT FACTS

HISTORY	YEAR	TEAMS
FIRST EDITION	1971/72	64
LATEST EDITION	2020/21	48 + 8*
NEXT EDITION	2021/22	32 + 8*

*Eight teams join the competition at the later knockout round

MOST WINS

SEVILLA — 6

MOST APPEARANCES

SPORTING LISBON — 34

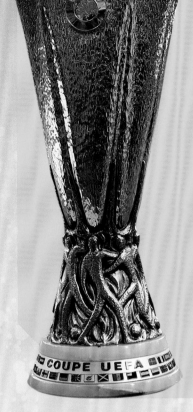

REYES' RECORD

The late Spanish winger José Antonio Reyes (below) won the UEFA Europa League trophy more times than any other player—twice with Atlético Madrid and three times with Sevilla.

SEVILLA'S FIESTA

Spanish club Sevilla have won more UEFA Europa League titles than any other team—five in total—including three trophies in a row between 2014 and 2016. Two of their victories have been decided by penalty shoot-outs.

The striking *Coupe UEFA* is the heaviest of all UEFA silverware. It has no handles, unlike UEFA's other men's trophies.

IFK Göteborg played 25 consecutive games in the UEFA Cup between 1980 and 1987 without a single loss, including their 1981–82 and 1986–87 winning campaigns.

SPANISH GLORY

Teams from Spain have set the pace in the competition, winning the trophy a record thirteen times. Sevilla, Atlético Madrid, Real Madrid, Valencia and Villarreal have all lifted the cup. Five different English teams have also been crowned champions.

KING HENRIK

Swedish striker Henrik Larsson remains the record goalscorer in the history of the competition with forty strikes (which includes goals he scored in qualifying rounds).

AWESOME EMERY

Spanish coach Unai Emery holds the record for the most UEFA Europa League wins. The Spaniard has won the title three times with Sevilla and most recently led Villarreal to their first title in 2021.

CONMEBOL LIBERTADORES

South America's major team competition is the CONMEBOL Libertadores, also known as the *Copa Libertadores*. Originally, only domestic champions could compete in the tournament. Now, a number of the top teams from each country can qualify to play in the tournament.

Brazilian side Palmeiras defeated Santos 1–0 at the Maracanã Stadium to win their second *Copa Libertadores* title in 2020.

Legendary Argentine coach Carlos Bianchi has won the trophy a record four times.

TOURNAMENT FACTS

MOST WINS	
INDEPENDIENTE	7

MOST APPEARANCES	
PEÑAROL	46
NACIONAL	46

HISTORY	YEAR	TEAMS
FIRST EDITION	1960	7
LATEST EDITION	2021	47
NEXT EDITION	2022	47

SANTOS SUPERSTAR

Brazil legend Pelé (right) is perhaps the most famous winner of the *Copa Libertadores* trophy. He twice won with Brazilian team Santos in 1962 and 1963.

GOALS GALORE

The record score for the biggest win in a game in *Copa Libertadores* history came in 1970 when Peñarol from Uruguay defeated Venezuelan side Valencia, 11–2!

EVER PRESENT

Paraguayan goalkeeper Ever Hugo Almeida, who twice won the competition as a player, holds the record for most games played. His 113 games for Club Olimpia from 1973 to 1990 may never be beaten.

COPA LIBERTADORES FEMENINA

The women's tournament has been contested annually since 2009, as women's soccer in South America continues to flourish. Brazil's São José lead the way with a hat-trick of titles—one of seven different teams to have been crowned champions. So far, teams from Brazil, Chile, Colombia, Paraguay, and Venezuela have reached the final.

FIFA CLUB WORLD CUP™

The FIFA Club World Cup™ was first held in 2000. This annual competition sees the champion teams from the six confederations recognized by FIFA, as well as the champions of the host nation, go head to head to determine the best team in the world.

Roberto Firmino's (right) goal secured Liverpool's place in FIFA Club World Cup™ history in 2019.

MOST WINS

👕	REAL MADRID	4

MOST APPEARANCES

👕	AL AHLY	6

TOURNAMENT FACTS

HISTORY	YEAR	TEAMS
FIRST EDITION	2000	8
LATEST EDITION	2020	6
NEXT EDITION	2021	7

HISTORY OF THE CUP

The Sir Thomas Lipton Trophy was an early international soccer tournament and a forerunner to the FIFA Club World Cup™. It was first contested in Italy between teams from England, Italy, Germany, and Switzerland in 1909.

INTERCONTINENTAL CUP

Between 1960 and 1979, the Intercontinental Cup was a two-game total-goals series, played by the winners of the UEFA's European Champion Clubs' Cup and the CONMEBOL's *Copa Libertadores*. From 1980 to 2004, the competition's format was changed to a one-off game, played in Japan.

Brazilian side Corinthians won the first FIFA Club World Cup™ in 2000.

Midfielder Toni Kroos (right) has won the FIFA Club World Cup™ five times—once with Bayern Munich and four times with Real Madrid.

PAST FIVE WINNERS	YEAR
BAYERN MUNICH	2020
LIVERPOOL	2019
REAL MADRID	2018
REAL MADRID	2017
REAL MADRID	2016

MORE FIFA TOURNAMENTS

YOUTH SOCCER

In addition to organizing international competitions for professional players, FIFA invests in the future of the game by running a number of global tournaments for young soccer players, both male and female.

FIFA U-20 WORLD CUP™

The FIFA U-20 World Cup™ has long been a stage on which many rising stars of the men's game have first emerged. The tournament has been staged biennially since 1977, when it was hosted by Tunisia and won by the Soviet Union (now Russia). Until 2005, the competition was known as the FIFA World Youth Championship. The first FIFA U-20 Women's World Cup™ was played in Chile in 2008.

FIFA U-20 WORLD CUP™ TOURNAMENT FACTS

MOST WINS		
ARGENTINA		6

MOST APPEARANCES		
BRAZIL		18

HISTORY	YEAR	TEAMS
FIRST EDITION	1977	16
LATEST EDITION	2019	24
NEXT EDITION	2023	24

Ukraine beat Korea Republic to win the FIFA U-20 World Cup™ in 2019.

FIFA U-20 WOMEN'S WORLD CUP™ FACTS

MOST WINS

🇩🇪	GERMANY	3
🇺🇸	USA	

MOST APPEARANCES

🇩🇪 🇺🇸	GERMANY / USA	9

HISTORY	YEAR	TEAMS
FIRST EDITION	2006*	16
LATEST EDITION	2018	16
NEXT EDITION	2022	TBC

*U-19 tournament was held in 2002 and 2004.

Japan claimed their first U-20 crown in 2018 with victory over Spain.

FIFA U-20 WOMEN'S WORLD CUP FRANCE 2018

FIFA U-17 WORLD CUP™

This competition started in 1985 as an under-16 tournament before switching to under-17 in 1991. Nigeria top the table with five tournament wins, while Brazil have four titles. The female edition has been played since 2008, with Spain the current champions and Korea DPR the only team to have won the trophy twice—in 2008 and 2016.

Argentina's Boca Juniors won the men's Blue Stars/ FIFA Youth Cup™ in 2019 in Zurich, Switzerland.

BLUE STARS/FIFA YOUTH CUP™

First launched back in 1939 by Zurich's oldest club FC Blue Stars, this yearly tournament brings together the best youth teams in the world, offering talented young players their first taste of international soccer. FIFA has been part of the tournament organization since 1991.

TOURNAMENT FACTS

MOST WINS

👕	MANCHESTER UNITED	18

MOST APPEARANCES

👕	FC BLUE STARS	81

HISTORY	YEAR	TEAMS
FIRST EDITION	1939	4
LATEST EDITION	2019	10
NEXT EDITION	2022	TBC*

*Yet to be announced at the time of print.

FUTSAL WORLD CUP™

Futsal is an indoor version of soccer, played on a hard court by teams of five. The game has had its own World Cup, organized by FIFA, since 1989. Brazil have won the competition a record five times. Lithuania will host the next contest of the tournament in 2021.

Argentina beat Russia 5–4 to win the FIFA Futsal World Cup™ in 2016.

MOST WINS	
🇧🇷 BRAZIL	5
MOST APPEARANCES	
SPAIN	
ARGENTINA	9

TOURNAMENT FACTS

HISTORY	YEAR	TEAMS
FIRST EDITION	1989	16
LATEST EDITION	2016	24
NEXT EDITION	2021	24

FIFA eWORLD CUP™

The FIFA eWorld Cup™ is virtual soccer's equivalent of the FIFA World Cup™. Each year the world's best gamers compete against each other in the FIFA video game series for the chance to win the FIFA eWorld Cup™.

Mohammed Harkous of Germany was the 2019 champion, choosing to play EA SPORTS FIFA 2019™ on the PS4.

The online viewing figures for the 2019 FIFA eWorld Cup™ Grand Final exceeded 47 million views on FIFA's viewing channels.

TOURNAMENT FACTS

HISTORY	YEAR	PLAYERS
FIRST EDITION*	2004	8
LATEST EDITION	2019	32
NEXT EDITION	2021	32

THE GRAND FINAL

Players from more than sixty countries around the world compete to earn one of the thirty-two places in the Grand Final. The format of the competition then follows that of the original edition of the FIFA World Cup™, with a group stage and knockout rounds before a head-to-head final showdown.

*Known as the FIFA interactive World Cup™.

THE BEST FIFA FOOTBALL AWARDS™

Held annually, The Best FIFA Football Awards™ recognizes players and coaches around the world for their achievements over a season. The event awards prizes to the best player, goalkeeper, and coach in both the men's and women's games.

Bayern Munich's ace goal scorer Robert Lewandowski was named The Best FIFA Men's Player for 2020.

The individual player awards used to be known as the FIFA World Player of the Year and the FIFA Women's World Player of the Year.

England's Lucy Bronze became the first-ever defender to collect The Best FIFA Women's Player award in 2020.

THE BEST FIFA MEN'S PLAYER

PLAYER	YEAR
ROBERT LEWANDOWSKI	2020
LIONEL MESSI	2019
LUKA MODRIĆ	2018
CRISTIANO RONALDO	2017
CRISTIANO RONALDO	2016

THE BEST FIFA WOMEN'S PLAYER

PLAYER	YEAR
LUCY BRONZE	2020
MEGAN RAPINOE	2019
MARTA	2018
LIEKE MARTENS	2017
CARLI LLOYD	2016

Bayern Munich's stopper Manuel Neuer is the most recent winner of the Best FIFA Men's Goalkeeper award.

Netherlands' coach Sarina Wiegman was named The Best FIFA Women's Coach for the second time in 2020.

TEAMS OF THE YEAR

Thousands of professional players from around the world vote to include their fellow players in the men's and women's FIFA FIFPRO World XIs. Eleven players earn a place in each team, which recognizes the game's most outstanding players in a season.

OTHER AWARDS

Three other prizes complete the list of annual awards. The FIFA Puskás Award is presented to the player, male or female, who scores the most beautiful goal of the calendar year, whereas the FIFA Fair Play Award honors sporting behavior that promotes the spirit of fair play, and the FIFA Fan Award rewards a special form of commitment and passion.

LIST OF HONORS
INTERNATIONAL TOURNAMENTS

FIFA WORLD CUP™ WINNERS

YEAR	COUNTRY
1930	URUGUAY
1934	ITALY
1938	ITALY
1950	URUGUAY
1954	WEST GERMANY
1958	BRAZIL
1962	BRAZIL
1966	ENGLAND
1970	BRAZIL
1974	WEST GERMANY
1978	ARGENTINA
1982	ITALY
1986	ARGENTINA
1990	WEST GERMANY
1994	BRAZIL
1998	FRANCE
2002	BRAZIL
2006	ITALY
2010	SPAIN
2014	GERMANY
2018	FRANCE

FIFA WOMEN'S WORLD CUP™ WINNERS

YEAR	COUNTRY
1991	USA
1995	NORWAY
1999	USA
2003	GERMANY
2007	GERMANY
2011	JAPAN
2015	USA
2019	USA

OLYMPIC GAMES – WOMEN'S WINNERS

YEAR	COUNTRY
1996	USA
2000	NORWAY
2004	USA
2008	USA
2012	USA
2016	GERMANY
2020*	

*Tokyo Games postponed until 2021 following the global outbreak of the COVID-19 virus in 2020.

OLYMPIC GAMES – MEN'S WINNERS

YEAR	COUNTRY	YEAR	COUNTRY
1900	GREAT BRITAIN	1972	POLAND
1904	CANADA	1976	EAST GERMANY
1908	GREAT BRITAIN	1980	CZECHOSLOVAKIA
1912	GREAT BRITAIN	1984	FRANCE
1920	BELGIUM	1988	SOVIET UNION
1924	URUGUAY	1992	SPAIN
1928	URUGUAY	1996	NIGERIA
1936	ITALY	2000	CAMEROON
1948	SWEDEN	2004	ARGENTINA
1952	HUNGARY	2008	ARGENTINA
1956	SOVIET UNION	2012	MEXICO
1960	YUGOSLAVIA	2016	BRAZIL
1964	HUNGARY	2020*	
1968	HUNGARY		

UEFA EUROPEAN CHAMPIONSHIP WINNERS

YEAR	COUNTRY	YEAR	COUNTRY	YEAR	COUNTRY
1960	SOVIET UNION	1984	FRANCE	2008	SPAIN
1964	SPAIN	1988	NETHERLANDS	2012	SPAIN
1968	ITALY	1992	DENMARK	2016	PORTUGAL
1972	WEST GERMANY	1996	GERMANY	2020*	ITALY
1976	CZECHOSLOVAKIA	2000	FRANCE		
1980	WEST GERMANY	2004	GREECE		

*UEFA European Championships held in 2021 following the global outbreak of the COVID-19 virus in 2020.

UEFA WOMEN'S CHAMPIONSHIP WINNERS

YEAR	COUNTRY	YEAR	COUNTRY	YEAR	COUNTRY
1984	SWEDEN	1993	NORWAY	2005	GERMANY
1987	NORWAY	1995	GERMANY	2009	GERMANY
1989	WEST GERMANY	1997	GERMANY	2013	GERMANY
1991	GERMANY	2001	GERMANY	2017	NETHERLANDS

CONMEBOL COPA AMÉRICA WINNERS

YEAR	COUNTRY	YEAR	COUNTRY	YEAR	COUNTRY
1916	URUGUAY	1942	URUGUAY	1989	BRAZIL
1917	URUGUAY	1945	ARGENTINA	1991	ARGENTINA
1919	BRAZIL	1946	ARGENTINA	1993	ARGENTINA
1920	URUGUAY	1947	ARGENTINA	1995	URUGUAY
1921	ARGENTINA	1949	BRAZIL	1997	BRAZIL
1922	BRAZIL	1953	PARAGUAY	1999	BRAZIL
1923	URUGUAY	1955	ARGENTINA	2001	COLOMBIA
1924	URUGUAY	1956	URUGUAY	2004	BRAZIL
1925	ARGENTINA	1957	ARGENTINA	2007	BRAZIL
1926	URUGUAY	1959	ARGENTINA*	2011	URUGUAY
1927	ARGENTINA	1963	BOLIVIA	2015	CHILE
1929	ARGENTINA	1967	URUGUAY	2016	CHILE
1935	URUGUAY	1975	PERU	2019	BRAZIL
1937	ARGENTINA	1979	PARAGUAY	2021	ARGENTINA
1939	PERU	1983	URUGUAY		
1941	ARGENTINA	1987	URUGUAY		

*There were two South American Championships in 1959. The other, known as the South American Championship 1959, was won by Uruguay.

COPA AMÉRICA FEMENINA WINNERS

YEAR	COUNTRY	YEAR	COUNTRY
1991	BRAZIL	2006	ARGENTINA
1995	BRAZIL	2010	BRAZIL
1998	BRAZIL	2014	BRAZIL
2003	BRAZIL	2018	BRAZIL

AFRICA CUP OF NATIONS WINNERS

YEAR	COUNTRY	YEAR	COUNTRY
1957	EGYPT	1990	ALGERIA
1959	UNITED ARAB REPUBLIC	1992	IVORY COAST
1962	ETHIOPIA	1994	NIGERIA
1963	GHANA	1996	SOUTH AFRICA
1965	GHANA	1998	EGYPT
1968	CONGO-KINSHASA	2000	CAMEROON
1970	SUDAN	2002	CAMEROON
1972	CONGO	2004	TUNISIA
1974	ZAIRE	2006	EGYPT
1976	MOROCCO	2008	EGYPT
1978	GHANA	2010	EGYPT
1980	NIGERIA	2012	ZAMBIA
1982	GHANA	2013	NIGERIA
1984	CAMEROON	2015	IVORY COAST
1986	EGYPT	2017	CAMEROON
1988	CAMEROON	2019	ALGERIA

AFC ASIAN CUP WINNERS

YEAR	COUNTRY
1956	KOREA REPUBLIC
1960	KOREA REPUBLIC
1964	ISRAEL
1968	IR IRAN
1972	IR IRAN
1976	IR IRAN
1980	KUWAIT
1984	SAUDI ARABIA
1988	SAUDI ARABIA
1992	JAPAN
1996	SAUDI ARABIA
2000	JAPAN
2004	JAPAN
2007	IRAQ
2011	JAPAN
2015	AUSTRALIA
2019	QATAR

AFRICA WOMEN CUP OF NATIONS WINNERS

YEAR	COUNTRY	YEAR	COUNTRY	YEAR	COUNTRY
1991	NIGERIA	2004	NIGERIA	2014	NIGERIA
1995	NIGERIA	2006	NIGERIA	2016	NIGERIA
1998	NIGERIA	2008	EQUATORIAL GUINEA	2018	NIGERIA
2000	NIGERIA	2010	NIGERIA		
2002	NIGERIA	2012	EQUATORIAL GUINEA		

AFC WOMEN'S ASIAN CUP WINNERS

YEAR	COUNTRY	YEAR	COUNTRY	YEAR	COUNTRY
1975	NEW ZEALAND	1991	CHINA PR	2006	CHINA PR
1977	CHINA PR	1993	CHINA PR	2008	KOREA DPR
1979	CHINESE TAIPEI	1995	CHINA PR	2010	AUSTRALIA
1981	CHINESE TAIPEI	1997	CHINA PR	2014	JAPAN
1983	THAILAND	1999	CHINA PR	2018	JAPAN
1986	CHINA PR	2001	KOREA DPR		
1989	CHINA PR	2003	KOREA DPR		

UEFA EUROPEAN CUP/CHAMPIONS LEAGUE WINNERS

YEAR	TEAM	YEAR	TEAM	YEAR	TEAM
1955–56	REAL MADRID	1977–78	LIVERPOOL	1999–2000	REAL MADRID
1956–57	REAL MADRID	1978–79	NOTTINGHAM FOREST	2000–01	BAYERN MUNICH
1957–58	REAL MADRID	1979–80	NOTTINGHAM FOREST	2001–02	REAL MADRID
1958–59	REAL MADRID	1980–81	LIVERPOOL	2002–03	AC MILAN
1959–60	REAL MADRID	1981–82	ASTON VILLA	2003–04	PORTO
1960–61	BENFICA	1982–83	HAMBURG	2004–05	LIVERPOOL
1961–62	BENFICA	1983–84	LIVERPOOL	2005–06	BARCELONA
1962–63	AC MILAN	1984–85	JUVENTUS	2006–07	AC MILAN
1963–64	INTERNAZIONALE	1985–86	STEAUA BUCHAREST	2007–08	MANCHESTER UTD
1964–65	INTERNAZIONALE	1986–87	PORTO	2008–09	BARCELONA
1965–66	REAL MADRID	1987–88	PSV EINDHOVEN	2009–10	INTERNAZIONALE
1966–67	CELTIC	1988–89	AC MILAN	2010–11	BARCELONA
1967–68	MANCHESTER UTD	1989–90	AC MILAN	2011–12	CHELSEA
1968–69	AC MILAN	1990–91	RED STAR BELGRADE	2012–13	BAYERN MUNICH
1969–70	FEYENOORD	1991–92	BARCELONA	2013–14	REAL MADRID
1970–71	AJAX	1992–93	MARSEILLE	2014–15	BARCELONA
1971–72	AJAX	1993–94	AC MILAN	2015–16	REAL MADRID
1972–73	AJAX	1994–95	AJAX	2016–17	REAL MADRID
1973–74	BAYERN MUNICH	1995–96	JUVENTUS	2017–18	REAL MADRID
1974–75	BAYERN MUNICH	1996–97	BORUSSIA DORTMUND	2018–19	LIVERPOOL
1975–76	BAYERN MUNICH	1997–98	REAL MADRID	2019–20	BAYERN MUNICH
1976–77	LIVERPOOL	1998–99	MANCHESTER UTD	2020–21	CHELSEA

UEFA WOMEN'S CHAMPIONS LEAGUE WINNERS

YEAR	TEAM	YEAR	TEAM	YEAR	TEAM
2001–02	FRANKFURT	2008–09	DUISBURG	2015–16	LYON
2002–03	UMEÅ	2009–10	TURBINE POTSDAM	2016–17	LYON
2003–04	UMEÅ	2010–11	LYON	2017–18	LYON
2004–05	TURBINE POTSDAM	2011–12	LYON	2018–19	LYON
2005–06	FRANKFURT	2012–13	WOLFSBURG	2019–20	LYON
2006–07	ARSENAL	2013–14	WOLFSBURG	2020–21	BARCELONA
2007–08	FRANKFURT	2014–15	FRANKFURT		

UEFA EUROPA LEAGUE WINNERS

YEAR	TEAM	YEAR	TEAM	YEAR	TEAM
1971–72	TOTTENHAM HOTSPUR	1990–91	INTERNAZIONALE	2011–12	ATLÉTICO MADRID
1972–73	LIVERPOOL	1991–92	AJAX	2012–13	CHELSEA
1973–74	FEYENOORD	1992–93	JUVENTUS	2013–14	SEVILLA
1974–75	BORUSSIA MÖNCHENGLADBACH	1993–94	INTERNAZIONALE	2014–15	SEVILLA
		1994–95	PARMA	2015–16	SEVILLA
1975–76	LIVERPOOL	1995–96	BAYERN MUNICH	2016–17	MANCHESTER UTD
1976–77	JUVENTUS	1996–97	SCHALKE	2017–18	ATLÉTICO MADRID
1977–78	PSV EINDHOVEN	1997–98	INTERNAZIONALE	2018–19	CHELSEA
1978–79	BORUSSIA MÖNCHENGLADBACH	1998–99	PARMA	2019–20	SEVILLA
		1999–2000	GALATASARAY	2020–21	VILLAREAL
1979–80	EINTRACHT FRANKFURT	2000–01	LIVERPOOL		
1980–81	IPSWICH TOWN	2001–02	FEYENOORD		
1981–82	IFK GÖTEBORG	2002–03	PORTO		
1982–83	ANDERLECHT	2003–04	VALENCIA		
1983–84	TOTTENHAM HOTSPUR	2004–05	CSKA MOSCOW		
1984–85	REAL MADRID	2005–06	SEVILLA		
1985–86	REAL MADRID	2006–07	SEVILLA		
1986–87	IFK GÖTEBORG	2007–08	ZENIT ST PETERSBURG		
1987–88	BAYER LEVERKUSEN	2008–09	SHAKHTAR DONETSK		
1988–89	NAPOLI	2009–10	ATLÉTICO MADRID		
1989–90	JUVENTUS	2010–11	PORTO		

COPA LIBERTADORES

YEAR	TEAM	YEAR	TEAM	YEAR	TEAM
1960	PEÑAROL	1981	FLAMENGO	2002	OLIMPIA
1961	PEÑAROL	1982	PEÑAROL	2003	BOCA JUNIORS
1962	SANTOS	1983	GRÊMIO	2004	ONCE CALDAS
1963	SANTOS	1984	INDEPENDIENTE	2005	SÃO PAULO
1964	INDEPENDIENTE	1985	ARGENTINOS JUNIORS	2006	INTERNACIONAL
1965	INDEPENDIENTE	1986	RIVER PLATE	2007	BOCA JUNIORS
1966	PEÑAROL	1987	PEÑAROL	2008	LDU QUITO
1967	RACING	1988	NACIONAL	2009	ESTUDIANTES
1968	ESTUDIANTES	1989	ATLÉTICO NACIONAL	2010	INTERNACIONAL
1969	ESTUDIANTES	1990	OLIMPIA	2011	SANTOS
1970	ESTUDIANTES	1991	COLO-COLO	2012	CORINTHIANS
1971	NACIONAL	1992	SÃO PAULO	2013	ATLÉTICO MINEIRO
1972	INDEPENDIENTE	1993	SÃO PAULO	2014	SAN LORENZO
1973	INDEPENDIENTE	1994	VÉLEZ SARSFIELD	2015	RIVER PLATE
1974	INDEPENDIENTE	1995	GRÊMIO	2016	ATLÉTICO NACIONAL
1975	INDEPENDIENTE	1996	RIVER PLATE	2017	GRÊMIO
1976	CRUZIERO	1997	CRUZEIRO	2018	RIVER PLATE
1977	BOCA JUNIORS	1998	VASCO DA GAMA	2019	FLAMENGO
1978	BOCA JUNIORS	1999	PALMEIRAS	2020	PALMEIRAS
1979	OLIMPIA	2000	BOCA JUNIORS	2021*	
1980	NACIONAL	2001	BOCA JUNIORS		

*The 2021 tournament is due to conclude in November.

COPA LIBERTADORES FEMENINA

YEAR	TEAM	YEAR	TEAM
2009	SANTOS	2016	SPORTIVO LIMPEÑO
2010	SANTOS	2017	AUDAX/ CORINTHIANS
2011	SÃO JOSÉ		
2012	COLO-COLO	2018	ATLÉTICO HUILA
2013	SÃO JOSÉ	2019	CORINTHIANS
2014	SÃO JOSÉ	2020	FERROVIÁRIA
2015	FERROVIÁRIA	2021*	

*The 2021 tournament is due to conclude in October.

INTERCONTINENTAL CLUB TOURNAMENT
FIFA CLUB WORLD CUP™

YEAR	TEAM	YEAR	TEAM
2000	CORINTHIANS	2013	BAYERN MUNICH
2005	SÃO PAULO	2014	REAL MADRID
2006	INTERNACIONAL	2015	BARCELONA
2007	AC MILAN	2016	REAL MADRID
2008	MANCHESTER UTD	2017	REAL MADRID
2009	BARCELONA	2018	REAL MADRID
2010	INTERNAZIONALE	2019	LIVERPOOL
2011	BARCELONA	2020	BAYERN MUNICH
2012	CORINTHIANS	2021*	

*The 2021 tournament is due to take place in December.

INDEX

Page references to images are in **bold**.